# MUSEUM WITHOUT WALLS

THE VOICES OF SILENCE

ANDRÉ MALRAUX

# Museum
# Without Walls

Translated from the French
by Stuart Gilbert and Francis Price

London
Secker & Warburg

Printed in France

*For Madeleine*

# TABLE OF CONTENTS

## INTRODUCTION

A Romanesque crucifix was not regarded by its contemporaries as a work of sculpture; nor Cimabue's *Madonna* as a picture. Even Phidias' *Pallas Athene* was not, primarily, a statue.

So vital is the part played by the art museum in our approach to works of art today that we find it difficult to realize that no museums exist, none has ever existed, in lands where the civilization of modern Europe is, or was, unknown; and that, even in the Western world, they have existed for barely two hundred years. They were so important to the artistic life of the nineteenth century and are so much a part of our lives today that we forget they have imposed on the spectator a wholly new attitude toward the work of art. They have tended to estrange the works they bring together from their original functions and to transform even portraits into "pictures." Though a bust of Caesar or an equestrian statue of Charles V may remain for us Caesar and the Emperor Charles, *Count-Duke Olivares* has become pure Velazquez. What do we care who the *Man with the Helmet* or the *Man with the Glove* may have been in real life? For us, their names are Rembrandt and Titian. The portrait has ceased to be primarily a likeness of an indi-

9

◀  1.  *Venice - Room in the Museo Correr.*

2.  *Téniers - The Gallery of the Archduke Leopold at Brussels.*

vidual. Until the nineteenth century a work of art was essentially a representation of something, real or imaginary. Only in the artist's eyes was painting specifically painting; and often, even to him, it was also a form of poetry. The effect of the museum is to suppress the model in almost every portrait (even that of a dream figure) and to divest works of art of their functions. It does away with the significance of Palladium, of saint and Savior; rules out associations of sanctity, qualities of adornment and possession, of likeness or imagination; and presents the viewer with images of things, differing from the things themselves, and drawing their *raison d'être* from this very difference. It is a confrontation of metamorphoses.

The reason the art museum made its appearance in Asia so belatedly (and, even then, only under European influence and patronage) is that, for an Asiatic, and especially the man of the Far East, artistic contemplation and the picture gallery are incompatible. In China, the full enjoyment of works of art necessarily involved ownership, except where religious art was concerned; above all it demanded their isolation. A painting was not exhibited, but unfurled before an art lover in a fitting state of grace; its function was to deepen and enhance his communion with the universe. The practice of confronting works of art with other works of art is an intellectual activity, and diametrically opposed to the mood of relaxation which alone makes contemplation possible. In Asiatic eyes, the museum may be a place of learning and teaching, but considered as anything else it is no more than an absurd concert in which contradictory themes are mingled and confused in an endless succession.

For over a century our approach to art has been growing more and more intellectualized. The museum invites comparison of each of the expressions of the world it brings together, and forces us to question what it is that brings them together. The sequence of seemingly antagonistic schools has added to the simple "delight of the eye" an awareness of art's impassioned quest, of a re-creation of the universe, confronting the Creation. After all, a museum is one of the places that show man at his noblest. But our knowledge covers a wider field than our museums. The visitor to the Louvre knows that it contains no significant representation of either Goya or of the great English artists, of Piero della Francesca or of Grünewald, of the paintings of Michelangelo or even those of Vermeer. In a place where the work of art no longer has any function other than that of being a work of art, and at a time when the artistic exploration of the world is in active progress, the assemblage of so many masterpieces—from which, nevertheless, so many are missing—conjures up in the mind's eye *all* of the world's masterpieces. How indeed could this mutilated possible fail to evoke the whole gamut of the possible?

Of what is it necessarily deprived? Until the present, at least, of such things as stained glass and frescoes, which form part of a whole; of objects, such as sets of tapestries, which are difficult to display; of everything that cannot be moved or cannot be acquired. Even when the greatest zeal and enormous resources have gone into its making, a museum owes much to opportunities that chance has thrown its way. Napoleon's victories did not enable him to bring the Sistine to the Louvre, and no art patron, however wealthy, will take to the Metropolitan Museum the Royal Portal of Chartres or the Arezzo frescoes. From the eighteenth to the twentieth century what migrated was the portable, with the result that far more Rembrandt paintings than Giotto frescoes have been offered for sale. Thus the art museum, born when the easel picture was the one living form of art, came to be a museum not of color but of paintings; not of sculpture but of statues.

In the nineteenth century the "grand tour" filled in the gaps left by the museums. But how many artists of the time were familiar with all of Europe's masterpieces? Gautier saw Italy (without seeing Rome) when he was thirty-nine; Edmond de Goncourt when he was thirty-three; Hugo as a child; Baudelaire and Verlaine, never. And yet Italy was the traditional heart of the "tour." They might have seen portions of Spain and Germany, and perhaps Holland; Flanders was relatively well known. The eager crowds that thronged the salons—composed largely of real connoisseurs—owed their art education to the Louvre. Baudelaire never set eyes on the master-pieces of El Greco, Michelangelo, Masaccio, Piero della Francesca, or Grünewald, Titian, or of Hals—or of Goya, though he had easy access to the Galerie d'Orléans. His *Phares* begins with the sixteenth century.

What had he seen? What, until 1900, had been seen by all those whose views on art still impress us as revealing and important; whom we take to be speaking of the same works, referring to the same sources, as those we know ourselves? Two or three of the great museums, and photographs, engravings, or copies of a handful of the masterpieces of European art. Most of their readers had seen even less. In the art knowledge of those days there existed an area of ambiguity: comparison of a picture in the Louvre with another in Madrid, in Florence, or in Rome was comparison of a present vision with a memory. Visual memory is not infallible, and successive periods of study were often separated by weeks of travel. From the seven-    11 teenth to the nineteenth century, pictures, interpreted by engraving, had *become* engravings; they had retained their drawing (at least relatively) but lost their colors, which were replaced by an interpretation in black and white; also, while losing their dimensions, they acquired margins. The nineteenth-century photograph was merely a more faithful print. The art lover of the time knew pictures in the same manner as we knew mosaics and stained-glass windows in the years preceding World War II.

Today, an art student can examine color reproductions of most of the world's great paintings and discover for himself a host of secondary works, as well as the archaic arts, the great epochs of Indian, Chinese, Japanese, and pre-Columbian sculpture, some Byzantine art, Romanesque frescoes, and primitive and "folk" art. How many statues could be seen in reproduction in 1850? Since sculpture can be reproduced in black and white more faithfully than painting, our contemporary art books have found in it a realm in which they are eminently successful. At one time, the student visited the Louvre and some subsidiary galleries and memorized what he saw as best he could. We, however, have far more great works available to refresh our memories than even the greatest of museums could bring together.

A museum without walls has been opened to us, and it will carry infinitely farther that limited revelation of the world of art which the real museums offer us within their walls: in answer to their appeal, the plastic arts have produced their printing press.

I

In answer to the appeal of the real museums—which echoed that of the real creators.... The art which invokes and governs this vast resurrection is not an art that can be easily defined; it is our own, and it is difficult for a fish to envisage the outer aspect of his aquarium. The arts it has revived all have a certain resemblance, but their realm is vaster than its own; the arts it has destroyed all have a certain resemblance, but their realm is more complex than any of their individual provinces. The victory of Piero della Francesca over Van Dyck, that of El Greco over Murillo, and that of the masters of Chartres and the Acropolis over the sculptors of Alexandria all took place at about the same time as the victory of Cézanne over the "official" painters of his day, and they have brought us to the realization that, if modern art and the museum without walls have been faced with powerful adversaries in official art, and even in the "esthetic of the past," it is primarily because this art and this esthetic derived legitimacy from a *general feeling:* from the will of all those who expected no more from painting than a privileged *spectacle.*

For five centuries—from the eleventh to the sixteenth—European artists, in Italy as in Flanders, in Germany as in France, concentrated their efforts on freeing themselves from a form of expression limited to two dimensions, and from what they took to be the clumsiness or ignorance of their predecessors. (Because of its use of an ideographic script executed with a hard brush, Far Eastern art had made much more rapid progress in mastery of its media.) In the sixteenth century the Europeans had discovered the secrets of rendering volume and depth and of creating the illusion of space.

Credit for the decisive technical advance belongs undoubtedly to Leonardo. In all previous painting—Greek vases or Roman frescoes, the art of Byzantium and the East, the Christian Primitives of various lands, the Flemish as well as the Florentines, the Rhenish as well as the Venetians—whether they were painting in fresco, in miniature, or in oils, painters had always composed *in terms of outlines.* By deliberately blurring outlines, then extending the limiting forms of objects into a distance which was no longer the abstract perspective of his predecessors (Uccello's and Piero's perspective emphasized rather than attenuated the isolation of objects) but a region where all

13

things seen were suffused in tones of blue, Leonardo, some years before Hieronymus Bosch, created and passed on a manner of rendering space such as Europe had never known before. No longer a mere neutral environment for bodies, his space flowed like time, enveloping figures and observers alike in its vast recession, and opening vistas on infinity. This space is not, however, just a hole in the picture surface, and even its transparency is still painting. Not until this discovery had been made could Titian break up his contour lines, or Rembrandt fulfill his genius in his etchings. But in Italy at that time it was necessary only to form a synthesis of Leonardo's technique and those elements of it which had been foreseen or employed by a few others—while carefully suppressing the transfiguration and intellect it expressed—in order to establish a semblance of accord between the painting and the world of ordinary vision in order for the forms to appear free of the confines of painting. To a viewer intent on illusion, a form depicted by Leonardo, Francia, or Raphael might have been more "lifelike" than one by Giotto or Botticelli, but no form in the centuries that followed would be more alive than Leonardo's; it would simply be different. At a time when Christianity, growing feeble and soon to be divided against itself, was ceasing to subject the testimony of man to that hieratic stylization which proclaims God's presence, the power of illusion Leonardo conferred on the artist was destined to change the whole course of painting.

Perhaps it is not a coincidence that, of all the great painters, the one who has had the most far-reaching and the least specific influence was one of the few for whom art was not his sole interest in life, his *raison d'être*.

When the academic tradition of the ancient world reappeared on the scene in the sixteenth century, seeming to carry with it a proclamation of the artistic value of sensual desire, the Christian world in general, and Italy in particular, was gradually, and not without setbacks, escaping from the domination of saints and demons. The "divine proportion" that governs the elements of the human body had become a law of art, and its ideal measurements were expected to govern all forms and images, just as they were considered to govern the movement of the planets.... That day when Nicolas of Cusa proclaimed: "*Christ is perfect man*," a Christian cycle closed, and with it the gates of hell; now Raphael's forms could come into being.

Italy and Flanders had taken it for granted that one of the primary functions of art was the creation of a semblance of reality. But what Italy sought was not so much the imitation of the real as the illusion of an idealized world. Italian art, concerned as it was with the techniques of imitation, and

14

3. *Filippo Lippi - Madonna (detail).*    4. *Leonardo da Vinci - Mona Lisa (detail).*

attaching so much importance to the "dimensionality" of its figures, aspired to a revelation of the unreal as well as to the most convincing expression of an enormous fiction—an imagined world of harmony.

All works of fiction begin with: "Let us suppose that...." The Monreale *Christ* had not been a supposition but an affirmation. Neither the Chartres *David* nor Giotto's *Meeting at the Golden Gate* had been suppositions. A *Virgin* by Lippi or by Botticelli had aspects of fiction; Leonardo's *Virgin of the Rocks* and *Last Supper* were sublime tales.

But until the sixteenth century, all progress in the creation of illusion had been linked to the creation or development of a style. If the archaic goddesses of Greece had been less illusory than those of the austere style, and these, in turn, less so than the young girls of Phidias; if Giotto's figures were less illusory than those of Masaccio, and Masaccio's less than Raphael's, their viewers had readily confused their creator's power of illusion with his genius, and based this genius on its power of illusion. The history of art imposed on Europe by Italy is reminiscent of a history of the applied sciences. No painter, no sculptor of the past was preferred to those of the present until the time of the rivalry between Leonardo, Michelangelo, Raphael, and, later, Titian: in other words, before possession by the artist of the techniques of illusion. Giotto was revered as a precursor, and so was Duccio, but until the nineteenth century no one would have thought of preferring their work to Raphael's; it would have been equivalent to preferring a sedan chair to an airplane. The history of Italian art was that of a series of discoverers, each with his own group of disciples.

The language of forms of Phidias or of the pediment of the temple of Zeus at Olympia had been as specific as that of the masters of Sumer or of Chartres, because, like it, it had been the language of a discovery. Its history, like that of Italian painting and sculpture, was a mingling of the conquest of illusion and of a progression toward the unknown. For more than three centuries, painting was to alternate between the maintenance of this demiurgic power—becoming a creation of the unreal as it had been a creation first of the gods and then of the world of God—and a means of representation of fiction, a technique for an imagined *tableau vivant*. Pascal's sentence: "What folly it is to admire a painting for its resemblance to things whose originals we do not admire at all!" is not a fallacy but an esthetic—meaning not so much that only beautiful things should be painted, but only such things as would be beautiful did they exist. From this esthetic stems the quest of ideal beauty.

Would it be more correct to term it rational beauty? Let us beware of its theorists. It represented not so much one esthetic among others as the esthetic of cultivated men who had no other. It still represents that.... It aspired to manifest itself in literature, in architecture, and, also, though more cautiously, in music. Above all, it sought to be transposable into life; sometimes very subtly. Since a Greek nude is more voluptuous than a Gothic one, would the Venus of Melos, if she came to life, be a beautiful woman? This concept of beauty was one on which men of culture could agree, even though they were indifferent to painting. A concept which made it possible to admire both picture and model *in the same way;* a concept called for by Pascal but only hinted at in the sharply etched, Rembrandt-like lines of his own style... A concept of beauty which maintained that a gallery should not be a gathering of paintings but a permanent display of carefully selected, imaginary spectacles.

For this art, which used reason as the basis for its claim to legitimacy, was the expression of a world created for the pleasure of the imagination. The very idea of beauty, in a civilization for which the human body is the principal object of art, is linked with the imaginary and with sensual desire, and forms to be admired in the abstract are easily confused with forms to be desired physically. The art that derived from this idea approached fiction with as much fervor as Romanesque sculpture had brought to faith, but the public for which it was intended confused Poussin with Le Sueur, and the quality of the painting with that of the spectacle it represented.

This public admired what it saw because of a mental attitude diametrically opposed to that which medieval art had required and modern art would require. There had been no more question of imagining the precursors of Christ as resembling the statue-columns of cathedrals than there is today of imagining Cézanne's bathers as resembling the image of them he has given us. In the taste of the seventeenth century, however, a picture's primary value stemmed from its projection into the imaginary of the forms it portrayed; and the more precise the suggestion conveyed by its forms the greater the value of the picture. The methods employed came to be those that would have permitted the subject, were it to come to life, to occupy a privileged place in the universe; in the world which art had "rectified" in order to stimulate admiration, and which painting now planned to rectify in order to stimulate the pleasure of the connoisseur—who was often less a connoisseur of painting than of fiction.

Thus, the mythological tales of Boucher were to take the place of those of Poussin.

All the more easily since painting had now come in contact with another potent realm of the imaginary: the theater. It occupied a position of ever-increasing importance in contemporary life: in literature, it was foremost; in the churches, it was imposing its style on religion. The Mass was disappearing beneath a weight of spectacle, just as the mosaics of the past were disappearing beneath a veneer of painting. To a church less concerned with the expression of faith than with the stimulation of piety, what form of painting could have been more effective than that which conveyed the highest form of illusion? Giotto had painted for the faithful as he would have painted for St. Francis of Assisi; the new painting was not meant for saints, and aspired less to bearing witness to faith than to seducing the masses. From this stems the violently secular nature of this art that purported to be so pious. Its sainted women were neither wholly saints nor wholly women. They had become actresses. And also from this stems the importance of 17 emotions and faces: the painter's principal means of expression had become the human personality. The *genre* scenes of Greuze were sisters to religious scenes. Where the later Gothic schools had created a vast passion play, this painting represented a vast opera; it considered itself a theater of the sublime. Thus, at the end of the eighteenth century, the esthetic of sentiment joined forces with that of reason: the mind was to be gratified by touching the heart. Stendhal's only reproach to the selections committee of the Salon was for its practice of rendering judgment on the basis of a rigid system—in other words, without sincerity—and he suggested that the committee be replaced by the Chamber of Deputies. Such a proposal, a century earlier, would have been equivalent to replacing it with the Court of Versailles. He was, in fact, simply endorsing the theory of the Jesuits and the Encyclopedists that good painting was that which was pleasing to all sincere and cultured men; and painting was pleasing to such men not to the extent to which it was painting but to the extent that it represented a fiction of high order. Stendhal loved Correggio for the delicacy and subtlety of his rendering of feminine emotions; the majority of his eulogies would apply, word for word, to a great actress —and some, indeed, to Racine. But everyone who is basically indifferent to painting instinctively projects pictures into real life and judges them in terms of the spectacle they suggest. In 1817 Stendhal wrote:

"Were we to attempt to list the components of ideal beauty, we would name the following forms of excellence: first, a look of very keen intelligence; secondly, gracefully molded features; thirdly, glowing eyes—glowing not with the dark fires of passion but with cheerful animation. The eyes give liveliest expression to the play of the emotions, and this is where sculpture fails. Thus modern eyes would be extremely candid. Fourthly, much gaiety; fifthly, great underlying sensibility; sixthly, a splendid form and, above all, the spritely grace of youth." He thought he was attacking David and Poussin; actually he was opposing one form of theater with another.

Barrès, eighty years later, will make no reference to ideal beauty. But he will certainly be in agreement with Stendhal in the matter of an ideology in which painting represents both fiction and culture. "I have not the least hesitation in ranking Guido, Domenichino, Guercino, the Carracci and their contemporaries, who give us such powerful and abundant analyses of passion, above the Primitives and even above the painters of the first half of the sixteenth century. I know that archaeologists delight in going back to the sources—to such painters as Giotto, Pisano, and Duccio. And I can understand why esthetes, enamored of the archaic and deliberately emasculating their virile emotions in quest of a more fragile grace, relish the poverty and pettiness of these minor artists. But anyone who judges for himself and refuses to be influenced by the pedantic prejudice in favor of sobriety, or by the fashions of the day—any man, in short, who is fascinated by the infi-

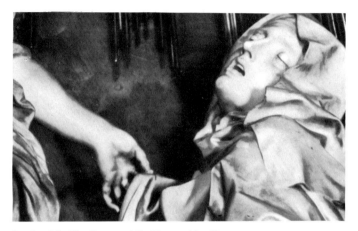

5. *Bernini - The Ecstasy of St. Theresa (detail)*.

nite diversity of the human soul—will recognize, in the good examples of seventeenth-century art in museums, the work of men whose driving force came, not from outside, but from within; men whose compositions are based, not on ancient statuary or models, but on their own emotions.

"Though modern taste disdains them, these artists often touch sublimity in dealing with the tender passions, and especially in the expression of intense sensual emotion. The element of pathos is heightened by a pathological veracity. We need only look at Bernini's famous statue of St. Teresa at Santa Maria della Vittoria in Rome. This is a great lady, swooning with love. Let us bear in mind the goals of the seventeenth and eighteenth centuries, as well as those of Stendhal and Balzac. Like them, these painters place their characters in situations which bring out precisely those sentiments of

◀ 6.   *Giotto - The Meeting at the Golden Gate (detail).*
7.   *Procaccini - The Penitent Magdalen and an Angel.*

embarrassment, perhaps, or helplessness—which are most apt to make us understand them, and to stir our feelings."

Barrès knew little of painting, but he loved pictures. He was aware of the transformation that was taking place in the museum. Confronted with the rediscovery of Giotto, he seemed to think that it was a matter of taste, a fashion of the moment which opposed Giotto's spectacles to those of the Carracci. Perhaps, however, he did sense that there was something else involved: that, to painters (and not, as he writes, simply to esthetes) the true value of painting does not reside in the faithful or idealized representation of spectacles. But he would have liked to see painting remain a succession of spectacles, and the painting of the past judged and admired for its quality as spectacle.

In his day, when the simultaneous impulse provided by new discoveries, by photography and by modern art was opening the doors of the museum without walls to the Primitives, "society" also would have liked to see painting remain spectacle. The fury aroused by *Olympia* had its roots, of course, in the belief that Manet did not know how to draw because "he does not imitate nature." (And perhaps, like Manet, Giotto imitates it poorly, but Duccio does not imitate it at all.) Society, which admired the minor masters of the Dutch school, did not reject realism because of its exactitude, but because of its vulgarity; the "distinction" these well-bred people demanded was inseparable from a form of theater, from a fiction of which painting was expected to be the principal exponent. Even to a writer as artistically knowledgeable as Walter Pater, painting was still fiction. The most powerful adversary of both the new museum and the new painting was neither a specific theory nor a specific school: it was this fiction, to which all generally admired paintings adhered.

The museum without walls will not become an accepted reality until modern art can destroy this fiction. But in the period between Stendhal's ideal beauty and Barrès' passionate beauty, an unprecedented event had taken place: the true artists had ceased to recognize the values of the ruling class.

The comic opera personage known as *le bourgeois* was born at the same time as his next-of-kin, the artist. But when the original comedy was discarded, the powerful bourgeoisie of Louis-Philippe and Napoleon III bore no more resemblance to the bourgeoisie of Louis XVI than Baudelaire to Racine or Van Gogh to Chardin.

The bourgeois king succeeded the last king of France to be anointed at

Rheims. The fundamental order imposed on the world by Christianity (and particularly by Catholicism, since Protestantism fosters neither cathedrals nor a Vatican) had disappeared. In losing its character of invulnerability, the basic order established by the great monarchies had also lost the legitimacy which the minor orders of the intellect derived from the order of the soul. The Goddess of Reason had failed in the attempt to found her own order: it would have been that of an exemplary Republic, and not the power of money or of techniques, which is not a right but a fact. David's concept of ideal beauty—Roman or Napoleonic—was a less satisfactory response to this Reason than Stendhal's, but even painters exasperated with the selections committee would have been unlikely to share Stendhal's desire to replace it with the Chamber of Deputies. Incapable of creating its own cathedrals and even its own palaces, forced to copy those of its predecessors, the new civilization was equally incapable of giving birth to a supreme expression of the world, a supreme expression of man.

Did the bourgeoisie have some vague hope that Ingres' message would do it the same service as Raphael's had done the papal aristocracy? But now there was no Julius II and, greatest lack of all, no Christ. Ingres' intellectual values were those suggested by Voltaire's tragedies. Like Sainte-Beuve, Ingres thought in terms of a vanished world; he would have been the ideal painter for a France that had not gone through a revolution and whose middle class had become what it was becoming in England, where the king remained the king. Like Balzac, he recast in the mold of the Restoration the vast social change going on around him; he swam against a tide that was sweeping in toward Daumier. After him, there were no great bourgeois portraits, though there still were some portraits in the grand manner, such as Delacroix's *Chopin* and Courbet's *Baudelaire*—but these are portraits of artists. If we dismiss such cases of "brotherly" accord, the portrait must finally belong to either the painter or the model, and they are enemies. *Madame Charpentier* is a Renoir, not the portrait of a lady of society, and the opposite is true of Bonnat's *Madame Cahen d'Anvers*. To realize this we have only to imagine these two pictures hung side by side in an 1890 drawing room. There were styles during the bourgeois epoch, but there was no great style of the bourgeoisie. Corot, who was basically a landscape artist, was the first to treat the human countenance as a landscape; soon the expression of the eyes, which had once meant so much, was to disappear.... And so much the worse for the model if it remained; the first ruling class that failed to find its portraitists very soon found its caricaturists.

23

8. *Ingres - Portrait of L.-F. Bertin.*
9. *Daumier - Gazan.*  ▶

Deprived of the stabilizing influence of the Christian monarchy and separated by more than time from the heroic age of the Convention, uneasily remembering the two revolutions that had raised him to power in the name of the people, and well aware that he himself was now threatened by both the people and by the resurgence of memories of Napoleonic glory (there would be a brief and superficial union of these two elements under the Second Empire), the French bourgeois asked no more of art than an imaginary world of illustration. His century—like the Victor Hugo of *Quatre-vingt-treize*—would have revolutionary myths and reactionary myths, but never a bourgeois myth. Throughout the eighteenth century the grip of the imaginary had been taking ever firmer possession of men's minds. The obsession with all things Roman had transformed the Revolution into a continuing spectacle whose actors were Roman heroes; but a day came when the imaginary ceased to be part of the living flesh of history, because it cannot exist on the level of contemporary events (except in the years of Apocalypse) because the unreal is a condition of its existence. Drawing on stories he had heard in his own family, Michelet wrote of "the vast boredom" of the Empire at its apogee, and many years would elapse before Napoleon's figure acquired its legendary glamor. Historical reincarnations began to lose their appeal: it would be more than sixty years before the Revolution regained, in literature, its Roman accent; neither 1848 nor the Commune were to regain the accent of the Convention. The only art of the imaginary that the victorious bourgeoisie called to life was one that rejected it. What did the bourgeoisie have in common with Delacroix's *Crusaders?* But the art that denied the bourgeois right of entry into the world of the imaginary welcomed into it everything that was opposed to him. The writings of a man such as Byron, an aristocrat in revolt against his country's aristocracy, stimulated the bourgeois artists of continental Europe in their revolt against the bourgeoisie. And the more this newly powerful middle class, unable to find in art a style with which it felt at home, came to ask of art a mere pleasure of the eye—switching over from a cult of Racine to a devotion to Augier, from glorification of Ingres to a passion for Meissonier—the more the artists, from Hugo to Rimbaud, from Delacroix to Van Gogh, broadened the scope of their revolt.

Confronted with a world in which practicality was the sole remaining force, Romanticism had called on the world of genius. The word genius had by no means the same connotations for the eighteenth century as it has for us today. Even to Stendhal, a man of genius was an ingenious—a powerfully original—man. The profound and mysterious resonance of the word, the very idea of a world of genius, is the offspring of Romanticism. Now Dante, Shakespeare, Cervantes, Michelangelo, Titian, Rembrandt, Goya became a frame of reference as definitive as Reason and classical antiquity once had been, although of a different nature. Art for its own sake was now recognizing and proclaiming its own heroes.

But the schism that separates the romantic writers from the classics does not have its equivalent in painting—except in the case of Goya, whose enormous influence would not be felt until a later period. The writers were opposed to both the classic literary esthetic, which was more or less accepted in the Europe of the seventeenth century, and to the works which expressed it; but, although the painters were also opposed to this esthetic, they were not opposed to the great works produced during its reign: *they continued them.* Racine is "in harmony" with Poussin, but who can be said to be in harmony with Hals or Velazquez or Rembrandt—all of whom, like Poussin, died in the years between 1660 and 1670? Though France dominated the literary values of the time, she did not dominate the painting of the time. Her classical literature is not contemporary with any classical painting, but with the great outburst of oil painting in Europe, which carried on the developments of the sixteenth century in Rome, and primarily in Venice. And Gericault, Constable, and Delacroix take their place in our museum in the same manner as their great predecessors. What line in any of their paintings would have been changed if they had never seen a cathedral? In the same sense in which Ingres is a neo-Roman, Delacroix is a neo-Venetian. In painting, Romanticism, opposing itself far less to a broad classicism than to a narrow neo-classicism, is not a style: it is a school. Its effect was not so much a modification of painting as a transformation of the inherited wealth of the museum, through an abrupt mutation of the values in which it had its roots.

The masters of this Western re-creation, to whom painting was a means of access to a cosmic or other-worldly realm, as it had sometimes been for those who preceded them a means of access to a sacred realm, have lost something of their influence today because the worst kind of painting has persisted in claiming descent from them; the theatrical is the caricature of the sublime. They have had less impact on modern art than El Greco, Vermeer, or Piero della Francesca but they still form a part of the highest spiritual values. Of our civilization and not simply of our romanticism: Why does the Michelangelo of Florence or the Rembrandt of his last works make us think of Beethoven rather than of Bach? The realm of art that once was theirs is a lost king-

10. *Rembrandt - The Three Crosses.*

dom today. It introduced into each form of art those things which are not limited by that art: Maillol would not have carved the Chartres *Kings* or the Rondanini *Pietà*, Mallarmé is not Shakespeare. But in the valley of the dead in which the nineteenth century placed Shakespeare beside Beethoven and Michelangelo beside Rembrandt, it linked them all with the heroes, saints, and sages. They were witnesses to a divine spark in man, and also the

11. *Michelangelo - Pietà Rondanini (detail)*. ▶

midwives to man as yet unborn. The great myths of the century—liberty, democracy, science, progress—converged on the greatest hope mankind had known since the days of the catacombs. When the tides of time have done their work of slow attrition and this fervent dream has joined so many others in the depths of oblivion, it will doubtless be recognized that none among them aspired as ardently as this one to confer on all men whatever greatness is man's due. But Rembrandt and Michelangelo will then be as close to Shakespeare as they are to Rubens, and far closer than they are to Fragonard or even to Velazquez—just as the transcendental element in certain of the mosaics of Monreale is as close to Dante as it is to Vézelay.

In the deep yet narrow chasm opened by these voices from the past, all of the past was being engulfed. And the simultaneous resurrection of these masterpieces separated the genius of their creators from the fiction through which they expressed it.

The masters of the unreal had been creators of *apparitions*. We know today that Italy discovered the *Venus* of Botticelli and of Titian, the figures in Raphael's *The School of Athens*, the *Sibyls* and the *David* of Michelangelo— although they were no longer figures of accepted truth—with the same stunned surprise with which France had discovered the angels of Rheims and the carved figures of the tympanum of Moissac and of the Royal Portal of Chartres; and with which Germany had discovered the *Horseman* of Bamberg, the regal women of Naumburg, and the crucifixes of the Rhineland. The character of conviction in these apparitions stemmed from an increasingly effective use of the means of illusion, but also from other means; those which belonged intrinsically to the act of creation. Any reasonably competent artist could paint illusory figures, but the creations of the unreal were figures in which great artists gave life—a life which was not ephemeral—to that which could only exist through them. Michelangelo's *David* had not been an illusory figure; the dogmatic freedom of Titian's last works had contained little element of concern for reproduction of actuality. Tintoretto's *St. Augustine Healing the Lepers* and his San Rocco *Crucifixion* are companions to Michelangelo's *Night*, the Barberini *Pietà*, and *The Burial of Count Orgaz* in a pantheon as far removed from theater as it is from the earth, in a solitude where they will be joined by Rembrandt. The most austere stylization in five centuries of Western art—that of El Greco—is founded on a language of swirling fabrics. In the Sistine Chapel *Last Judgment*, in Titian's *Pietà*, even in the San Rocco *Crucifixion*, the over-all patterns of color form a stormy monochrome as hostile to seduction and illusion as the dazzling *St. Augustine*

12. *Tintoretto - St. Augustine Healing the Lepers.*

*Healing the Lepers*, the richest examples of Titian, or the *Martyrdom of St. Maurice* in the Escorial. Rubens painting for himself is less dramatic, but abandons the forms of opera for a passionate world of spirits, for landscapes more brilliant, more idealized than any previously known to painting.

All of these apparitions had become spectacles because nineteenth century society saw a *Venus* of Titian in the same light as those of Cabanel, because it confused those of Cabanel with those of Titian. But while the esthetic of fiction was extending its sway across two thirds of Europe, painting, with Velazquez, with Rembrandt, had continued its pursuit of its own destiny. Gone were the admiration and understanding that, to one degree or another, had greeted the work of all the great artists, from Cimabue to Raphael and Titian: the aging Rembrandt is the first of the scorned and neglected geniuses. Until the sixteenth century, painters had participated in the fiction of their times and their discoveries had given it a new profundity; later, secondary painters participated in it without discovering anything; and, finally, the masters went on with their discoveries without participating. From this point on, for the painters and for some portion of the knowledgeable public— aided by Delacroix, who gave new life to Venice and provided a continuity for Rubens, and by the introduction of photography and the consequent decrease in value of the techniques of illusion—these spectacles ceased to be spectacle. They did not again become apparitions, but became pictures, in the sense in which we understand that word today. To the real artists, they had always been this; but not always *as a whole*. Although Delacroix admired Raphael, Ingres condemned Rubens. The long conflict between the advocates of Poussin and those of Rubens would, in the future, be a pointless debate. Just as Romanticism had substituted, for a style which was thought to be exemplary, a heroic creation that, in its own turn, seemed beyond the reach of history, so Manet and the fledgling forms of modern art would now open the way to a specifically pictorial creation detached from the legacy of the past.

## II

Manet progressed from his first romantic canvases to *Olympia*, to the *Portrait of Clemenceau*, and to the small *Bar des Folies-Bergère*, just as painting progressed from the academic tradition of the museums to modern art. And in doing so, he provided us with a guide to those elements from the traditional past that seem called on to figure in the new museum: his progenitors were to be its acknowledged masters. To begin with, of course, Goya.

Goya foreshadows all modern art, but painting is not in his eyes the supreme value: its task is to cry out the anguish of man forsaken by God. The seemingly picturesque elements in his work are never gratuitous and are linked — as great Christian art was linked with faith—to age-old collective emotions that modern art has chosen to ignore. His *Shootings of May Third* voices the outcry of suffering Spain; his *Saturn*, mankind's oldest cry. The element of the fantastic in his work does not come from albums of Italian *capricci*, but from the depths of man's fears; like Young, like most of the pre-Romantic poets, but with consummate genius, he gives voice to the powers of the night. What is modern in him is the freedom of his art. His colors may not be derived from Italy, but they are not always unrelated to those of the museum: we can imagine a dialogue between the tragic darkness of the *May Third* and the darkness of Rembrandt, but not with that darkness which, after Manet, will be no more than another color. There is no great distance between the *Majas on the Balcony* and Murillo's *Young Girl and Her Duenna;* but what of the distance from these *Majas* (still rather innocent) to Manet's *The Balcony?* A modern anthology can be assembled from Goya's work, as it can from Victor Hugo's; but how would it be possible not to hear in it the voice from the depths?

With the rediscovery of Goya and of Velazquez, the last works of Frans Hals reappear (the hands in *The Women Governors* strike perhaps the first aggressively modern note in painting); in Goya's drawings we are again made aware of the sketches in which the aging Titian broke peremptorily with the continuing line of Florence and of Rome; and, finally, we are newly conscious of the glory of Rembrandt. This lineage is shared, though not so obviously, by some of the Venetians, the Spanish, the English portraitists (in spite of Thoré, Vermeer will make a belated appearance); and later by Gros, Geri-

◀ 13. *Murillo - Young Girl and Her Duenna.*

14. *Manet - The Balcony.*

cault, Delacroix, Constable, Turner, and Courbet—even by Decamps and Millet.

But what we see in these artists is some specific accent of the work rather than the work itself, because they are often telling a story. And the prime characteristic of modern art is that it does not tell a story.

Before it could be born, the art of fiction had to die. And it did not die easily. The great theme of history in painting declined steadily throughout the eighteenth century, although it retained a position of dominance shared only by the portrait. There was nothing to retard the movement as it was carried on through the fantasies and ballets of Watteau to the anecdote and the still life, to Chardin, to the boudoirs and gardens of Fragonard (and *L'Enseigne de Gersaint* is a *genre* picture, an anecdote in oils). There was a

momentary revival with David, with Gros; and lastly with Delacroix. Then came the end. Delacroix, in *Liberty Guiding the People*, and Manet, in *The Execution of the Emperor Maximilian*, tried to instill new life into historical painting, but after *Maximilian* Manet never made another attempt. Though Courbet did not wish to tell a story but to depict something different from what his predecessors had depicted, he too aimed at representation—and this is why in our eyes he belongs to the traditional museum. When he replaced Delacroix's subjects with *The Funeral at Ornans* and *L'Atelier*, he was combating the museum in as superficial a manner as was Burne-Jones when he painted Botticellian subjects or as Gustave Moreau when he painted unicorns; and his genius is not related to this substitution. The truth was that the "subject" was bound to disappear, because a new subject was coming to the fore to the exclusion of all others, and this new subject was the presence of the artist himself upon his canvas. To realize his *Portrait of Clemenceau* Manet had to dare to be everything in the portrait, and Clemenceau next to nothing.

We know now what Clemenceau thought of this portrait: "I'm missing one eye and my nose is askew." He meant it as a joke, because it was he who sponsored the admission of *Olympia* to the Louvre. It was a different form of disagreement from that which brought him into conflict with Rodin. He had demanded that the sculptor redo his bust, because he objected to the interpretation of his face: it would be hard to imagine such an argument between Donatello and one of his models. Clemenceau felt that Clemenceau according to Rodin should also be Clemenceau according to himself. But in the portrait it was not simply a matter of Clemenceau according to Manet: it was primarily a matter of Clemenceau according to painting as such.

In spite of the debt to his juniors implicit in a part of his work, and in spite of the renown of his senior, Daumier, the name of Manet has acquired a symbolic meaning. He was dead when Cézanne declared: "*Our Renaissance dates from Olympia*," and Degas said: "*He was greater than we had thought him to be*." But it was at his exhibitions that the conflict which marks the origin of modern painting became pronounced, for it was here that values were publicly proclaimed that, until now, had been concealed. Daumier, embarrassed by his own genius, painted more for his own satisfaction than for posterity. Like Goya, he belongs to both the museum and to modern art. His paintings of everyday subjects *(The Washerwoman, The Evening Meal)* are in no sense anecdotes; the strugglings and poverty of the people are here

17. *Manet - Portrait of Clemenceau.* ▶

transformed by his art, just as they are, in history, by his friend Michelet. His illustrative subjects *(The Thieves and the Donkey, Don Quixote)* are more than mere illustration, his Dutch studies (seated players, collectors of prints and paintings) are more than mere anecdote—to such an extent that the viewer fails to realize that the subject is Dutch—because of their breadth of style, the indifference to any form of illusion, and a schematic composition that is unmistakably modern. But modern artists were destined to part company with him, as they did with Goya, because of their rejection of all values that are not intrinsically those of painting, and because of the nature of their palette.

◀  18. *Goya - The Burial of the Sardine.*

19. *Daumier - The Chess-Players.*

20. *Goya - The Shootings of May* 3, 1808.

Manet's *Execution of Maximilian* is Goya's *May Third*, without what the latter signifies. *Olympia* is the *Maja Desnuda*, just as *The Balcony* is the *Majas on the Balcony*, without the significance of these two Goyas. The devil's emissaries have become innocent portraits. A Manet washerwoman would have been the same as Daumier's, without what the latter signifies; simply a relative of *The Woman in the Laundry*. The direction Manet was attempting to set for painting rejects such significances. And their exclusion is linked, in his work, with the creation of a dissonant harmony that is echoed in all of modern painting.

Daumier's *The Chess Players* has little more significance than most of Manet's canvases, but the faces in it are still expressive; it is not mere chance that Manet was primarily a great painter of still lifes. The harmony of *The Chess Players*, striking as it is, forms a part of the structural system of the museum. Manet's contribution, not superior but radically different, is the green of *The Balcony*, the pink patch of the dressing gown in *Olympia*, the touch of red behind the black bodice in the small *Bar des Folies-Bergère*. His temperament, as well as his deference to the prestige of the museum, led

21. *Manet - The Execution of the Emperor Maximilian.*

him at first to seek to construct his forms with a profusion of Spanish-Dutch browns that were not shadow, contrasting them with clear colors that were

43

not light; it was a reconciliation of tradition with a pleasure of painting. Later, the closer relationship between colors, increasingly free of browns and glazes, assumed its specific character. *Lola de Valence* was not quite "a black and pink jewel," but *Olympia* marked a step in this direction, and in Cézanne's *A Modern Olympia* the enveloping darkness has disappeared. Manet's black cat was almost lost in shadow, Cézanne's black cat is silhouetted against the sheets. And in Cézanne's *Still Life with Clock*, the marble clock is actually black and the big conch shell is actually pink. This new harmony

45

◀ 22. *Manet - Olympia (detail)*.

23. *Cézanne - A Modern Olympia*.

24. *Cézanne - Still Life with Clock.*

*of colors among themselves* replacing a harmony of colors and darknesses, which was a part of the realm of illusion, led directly to the use of pure color. The darknesses of museum art were not the garnet reds of the fifteenth century, but those of the *Virgin of the Rocks:* tones born of depth and shadow. And shadow had served to temper the deliberately harsh discords of many Spanish paintings. Now, with the disappearance of shadow, these tones also disappeared: the employment of a dissonant harmony, timidly at first, paved the way for the resurrection of two-dimensional painting. From Manet to Gauguin and Van Gogh, from Van Gogh to the Fauves, this dissonance was to strengthen its claims to legitimacy, and to develop finally the harshness of the forms of the New Hebrides. In an age when pure color was on the point of disappearing in France, along with the traditional folk prints and sculpture, it became a part of a highly sophisticated form of painting that seemed destined to provide a mysterious link with the past. It was to have a profound influence on the transformation of the museum.

What did the museum include at that time? Ancient art, more Roman than Greek; Italian painting beginning with Raphael; the Dutch and Flemish masters; the Spaniards beginning with Ribera; Franch artists after the seventeenth century, and English after the eighteenth; Dürer and Holbein rather in the background; and still further in the background, a few Primitives.

It was essentially a museum of painting in oils; of a kind of painting in which the conquest of the third dimension had been all-important and for which a synthesis of illusion and pictorial expression was a *sine qua non*. A synthesis that aspired to portrayal of not only the form of things but of their volume and texture (disregarded in all arts other than those of the West); in other words, to a simultaneous impact on sight and touch. A synthesis, moreover, that did not attempt to suggest space as an infinitude, in the manner of Chinese wash drawings, but to limit it to the confines of a frame and to immerse objects in it as fish are immersed in the water of an aquarium. It is this that was the origin of the constant search for a particular light, a specific angle of illumination: in the entire world, and ever since man has painted, only Europe has known the shadows that are a part of our paintings. Such a synthesis often resulted in a corresponding union between what we see and touch and what we know. From this stems the *linking of detail with depth*, which occurs in no other art but ours.

In pursuit of this synthesis, which seemed destroyed each time it was surpassed, Western painting had made a series of discoveries. We have already observed that a Giotto fresco looked more "true to life" than one by Cavallini, a Botticelli painting more real than a Giotto, and a Raphael more real than a Botticelli. In the Low Countries as in Italy, in France as in Spain, seventeenth-century artists applied all of their genius to research in this direction, and the now general use of oils was at once a symptom of and a powerful adjunct to their quest. The rendering of movement, light, and texture had been mastered; techniques such as foreshortening, chiaroscuro, and the manner of painting velvet had been discovered, and each successive discovery had promptly been incorporated into the common stock of knowledge, just as the devices of *montage* and the traveling shot have become common practice in the cinema arts of today. It followed naturally that illusion should become the supreme form of expression and the criterion of value, as it had been in what was then termed the art of antiquity. And from this, in turn, came the accepted practice of subordinating the execution of the picture to what it represented.

In the museum, which was no less ignorant of the archaic arts and of the Temple of Zeus at Olympia than it was of fetishes, and where Michelangelo's most profound works were considered unfinished, Greek art—all art, in fact—began with Phidias. The "finish" thus became a characteristic of all accepted sculpture—which is to say, of antique sculpture—and of all European sculpture after Donatello's *David:* Romanticism exalted the poetically picturesque quality of the cathedrals, but Viollet-le-Duc felt that he would be saving Notre-Dame de Paris by destroying its statues. And "finish" is also a characteristic of almost all museum painting. But the primary common characteristic of the arts whose resurrection was now discreetly beginning is the absence—the refusal—of finish. Hence the discovery, summed up by Baudelaire speaking of Corot, that "a complete work was not necessarily finished, a finished work not necessarily complete."

What is referred to in the language of artists as "execution" then took the place of "rendering." It was said that Manet did not know how to paint a centimeter of flesh, and that *Olympia* was drawn in wire, but those who said it neglected the primary fact that, before the thought of drawing *Olympia* or of painting flesh, Manet wanted to paint pictures. Lighting was the least of his concerns. (Incidentally, in *Olympia* and in *Le Fifre* does the light really come from directly in front?) The pink robe in *Olympia*, the raspberry splash of the balcony in the small *Bar des Folies-Bergère*, the blue fabric in the *Déjeuner sur l'Herbe*, are obvious areas of *color*, in which the basic matter is pictorial, not represented or rendered. The picture, whose depths had once been those of a pit, becomes a surface. Even the most forceful of Delacroix's sketches were dramatizations: what Manet undertakes in some of his canvases is a translation of the world into terms of painting.

From this point on, the will of the artists decreed that painting should take clear and visible precedence over spectacle, instead of apparently being subordinated to it, and it seemed to them that they had found a foreshadowing of this precedence (not in any planned manner and employed in a whole body of work, but accidentally, often limited to a small area, a single canvas, a sketch for a later work, and always subordinate) in the work of those masters who "drew with a brush."

Rubens, with the heavy, irregular arabesques of his sketches; Hals, with those stylized hands that made him a prophet of modern art; Goya, with his accents of pure black; Delacroix and Daumier, with their tempestuous whiplashes of paint—all seemed intent on stamping their canvases with their own personalities, resembling in this the Primitives, who added their own portraits to those of the donors. Their impetuous drawing, which was often allied with a relative independence of areas of color, was in fact a signature. And the painters who signed their work thus seemed to have been more concerned with the medium itself than with what it represented.

Yet both medium and drawing remained at the service of representation. In Titian's last works and in the art of Tintoretto, the accent of the brush, the readily apparent line are instruments of expression of a dramatic lyricism; and the same is true of Rembrandt, though his lyricism lies beneath the sur-

25. *Manet - Study for the Bar des Folies-Bergère.*

26. *Magnasco - Convicts in Prison.*

face. It was not without qualms that Delacroix indulged himself in the fierce liberties of Rubens at his stormiest. Goya occasionally went further than any of the others; but if we exclude his "voices" and the influence of the shadows he inherited from the museum, Goya is modern art.

27. *Fragonard - Portrait of the Abbot of Saint-Non (?)*.

There was also Magnasco, Fragonard, and one element of Guardi. The frenetic line in the best Magnascos resembles a series of exclamation points, seeming to follow the play of a light that borders the contours of objects and figures (that "fringe of light" which Ingres thought incompatible with the dignity of art). This light always serves his purpose; even when he does not represent it, the brush strokes follow its unseen ripples. In Magnasco's work, as in that of greater masters—Tintoretto or Rubens—the elaborate brushwork subordinated fiction to painting because it diminished the sense of illusion; but his dazzling Italian tragicomedy was too often carried to extremes. And the power in his work that was admired by the painters who knew it, the same power so many others admired in the last Titians—and especially in Rubens and Rembrandt, who were known to everyone—constituted a form of legacy from these masters to the eighteenth century. Sometimes it was recognized and claimed, but even when it was not—Watteau, Fragonard, the English, Guardi, Goya—artists rediscovered it, freed of its dross of concessions, in a realm that was almost private and confidential: that of the sketch.

In principle, a sketch is a "state" of a work, prior to its completion and especially to the final execution of its details. But there is also a particular kind of sketch: that in which the artist, oblivious to the spectator and indifferent to illusion, reduces a perceived or imagined scene to its purely pictorial content—an aggregate of patches, colors, movements.

There is often failure to distinguish between the two kinds of sketch: the working sketch (or study) and the sketch that records the artist's direct "raw" impression—just as there is confusion between the Japanese sketch and the great synthetic art of Far Eastern wash drawings; and between the preparatory sketches of Degas or Toulouse-Lautrec and the draftsmanship of some of their lithographs, which often seem to have been dashed off on the impulse of the moment. The rough sketch is a memorandum; the expressive sketch is an end in itself. And being an end in itself, it differs essentially from the completed picture. An artist such as Delacroix or Constable, when completing certain sketches, did not set out to improve on them but to interpret them—by adding details allied with depth, so that (in Delacroix's case) the horses became more like real horses, and (in Constable's case) the hay-wain more literally a haywain, while the picture came to be as much an actual

53

31. *Delacroix - The Sultan Mulay Abd er-Rahman Receiving the Count de Mornay (sketch)*.

scene or a "story" carrying conviction as a work of art. Thus it achieved the sense of illusion by means of that "finish" intended for the spectator; a mere survival, in such cases, of elements the sketch had rejected.

Artists knew this very well, and were beginning to recognize it ever more clearly. The sketches which the greatest painters had marked for preservation (those of Rubens, for instance, and Velazquez' *Gardens*) do not strike us as unfinished pictures but as complete pictorial expressions which would lose much of their vigor, perhaps all, if they were subjected to the techniques of representation. Though Delacroix maintained the superiority of the finished picture, it was no mere accident that he preserved a large number of his sketches, whose quality *as works* is equal to that of his best pictures. He remembered Donatello's rough-hewn studies, and Michelangelo's; and he was well acquainted with the "unfinished" *Day*. Nor is it due to mere chance that Constable, first of the great modern landscape painters, carried out some of his most important canvases in "the style of a sketch" before painting the so-called completed versions. The latter he exhibited, while practically hiding away those wonderful sketches, of which he wrote that *they* were the real pictures. It is fortunate also that Valenciennes preserved the studies that reveal him to us today as Corot's precursor, a very different artist from the official painter of whose work nothing would remain if the sketches did not exist. And Daumier ...

Not that the sketch was considered, by its very nature, to be superior to the completed work. This was a matter of sketches of a particular kind, in the category of Leonardo's *Adoration of the Magi*, of some "unfinished"

32. *Valenciennes - Roof in Sunlight.*

33. *Delacroix - The Battle of Taillebourg.*

Rembrandts, and of almost all of Daumier. It is doubtful that Raphael's sketches for portraits belonged in this category, and Ingres' sketch for his *Stratonice* is inferior to the painting at Chantilly; but these are sketches which are preparations, *states* of the painting, and must therefore conform with the laws of the painting itself. Rubens' sketches are not, however, simply states of another work, and Delacroix's sketch for *The Battle of Taillebourg* conforms with Delacroix's laws, while the completed picture seeks to establish a conformity with both the accepted criteria of his day and with the testimony of our senses; with the traditional illusionism which Delacroix, in his journal, never dared reject completely. The treatment of the stone blocks in the foreground of the completed *Battle* caters to the popular taste to such an extent that the entire work becomes almost a typical example of Salon painting. Delacroix preserved his sketches; Corot, like Constable, kept in his studio and never exhibited the youthful works which would later find an echo in the work of his purist, most individual style. Art was entering into conflict with "finish," with the testimony of our senses, with painting considered as a representation of spectacle.

And the dividing line between the sketch and the picture was becoming

34. *Delacroix - The Battle of Taillebourg (sketch)*.

35. *Rembrandt - The Night Watch (detail)*.

less clearly defined. In many acknowledged masterpieces, in some Venetian works, in the last paintings of Hals, and in many English pictures whole passages were treated in the manner of a sketch. Is Rubens' *Philopoemen* a sketch or a picture? And what of some Rembrandts? And, far closer to the artists of this new age, Corot's *Marietta* and the first version of the *Pont de Narni*, as well as the finest paintings of Daumier, of Carpeaux, of Monticelli? For Corot, as for Valenciennes, Constable, Géricault, Delacroix, and Daumier, the style of the sketch was the form of freedom—a freedom that was being more and more eagerly pursued, even though the pursuit was accompanied by qualms of conscience.

*36. Daumier - Mother Holding Her Child.* ▶

37. *Delacroix - Lion Hunt (sketch)*.

These qualms were soon to vanish. Delacroix, although he loved and preserved his sketches, did not equate them with his finished pictures. Cézanne admired these same pictures in spite of their finish, in spite of their subject, and *for* the sketch secreted behind them; and he admired the actual sketches for themselves. In Delacroix he revered "the most beautiful palette in Europe." What artists retained from their predecessors who drew with a brush, what they retained from Turner, from the sketches of Rubens and of Fragonard, was the refusal to imitate others and a new strength of color—a color in which that of the spectacle represented ceases to be the apparent model and becomes the instrument.

It was this that provided the foundation for the adventure of impressionist *ideology*. To critics and jurists, all impressionist paintings seemed to be sketches. To Claude Monet, and to those who felt as he did, these sketches were rooted in spectacle and expressed it with greater intensity than the paintings of their predecessors. Spectacle is unquestionably here, expressed in a poetic sensitivity to fog, to snow, to springtime; and primarily, of course, to light. But Impressionism is not a school of *plein air* painting brought to perfection by a group of opticians. Although the public of the time found it impossible to determine what they represented, these pictures, which were destined to become symbols of the true-to-life (and especially when they depict, as they so often do, spectacles that have now disappeared: Pissarro's *Boulevards*, Renoir's *Avenue de l'Opéra*), state themselves clearly as impressions—which is simply another way of saying interpretations. But however individual they may be, these interpretations are not governed by a form of imitation—we might even say "hyperimitation"—which would be to a landscape what idealization or caricature are to the human form. They are governed by "painting": by a quest for the intensity of colors, and a correlation of these colors, in the name of the newly proclaimed primacy of the artist over what he depicts. The theorists of Impressionism asserted that painting appeals primarily to the eye; but if the paintings they defended appeal to the eye, it is far more as paintings that they do so than as landscapes. Even as the relationship between the artist and nature was changing, these theorists were analyzing *in terms of nature* what the artists were doing—not always in a deliberate manner, but with an admirable continuity of purpose—*in terms of painting*.

How often the relationship between theory and practice has become a kind of comedy played out in the mind! Artists construct theories as to what they would like to do, and do what they are capable of doing; but their ability, though in some cases too feeble for their theories, is in other cases stronger than those theories. The work that most clearly conforms with the theories Hugo set down in his preface to *Cromwell* is certainly not his own *Ruy Blas;* it is undoubtedly Claudel's *L'Annonce Faite à Marie*. Courbet's theories are ludicrous when confronted with his paintings. It is of no importance that the banks of the Seine should be more true to nature in the work of Sisley than in that of Théodore Rousseau; what the new art sought was a reversal of the relationship between object and picture, the manifest subordination of the object to the picture. Just as Delacroix had preserved his sketches for the admiration of Cézanne, Monet was to preserve his last

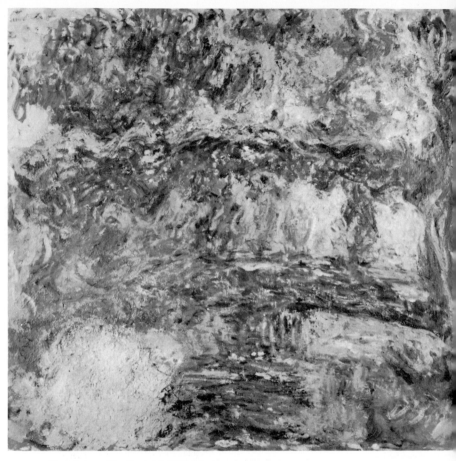

38. *Monet - The Japanese Bridge.*

*Nymphéas*, which are far more audacious than those in the Orangerie, for the admiration of the *tachistes* of 1950. In the work of Renoir, Gauguin, Ensor,

Van Gogh, there are many instances in which all that remains of their Impressionism is the intensity of color. At the end of the century, the vivid spots of color (the *taches*) of Bonnard and Vuillard were pictorial and not impressionist. The division of tones leads to pure color, and not in any way to a more subtle "vision." At a later period, when the Fauves appeared on the scene, all ambiguity was to beswept away and the arbitrary right of the painter recognized.

Manet was born in 1832, Pissarro in 1830, Degas in 1834; in the two years between 1839 and 1841 Cézanne, Monet, Rodin, Redon, and Renoir were born, and to each of them the visible world was to become the alphabet of his own language. The eye that saw this world was no more than a means to an end, and this end was the transposition of things seen into a pictorial universe, coherent, autonomous, and personal. And it would not be long before Van Gogh was painting. Representation of the world was to be followed by its annexation.

39. *Vlaminck - Interior.*

The description of the new art as "the world as viewed by a temperament" is false, for it is not just a way of seeing: Cézanne did not see objects in terms of their volume, nor Van Gogh in wrought iron, any more than the Byzantine painters saw in terms of ikons or Braque would see fruit dishes in separate fragments. The new art is, rather, the annexation of forms by means of an inner pattern or schema, which may *or may not* take the shape of objects, but of which, in any case, figures and objects are no more than the expression. The artist's supreme aim became that of subjecting all things to his own creation, beginning with the simplest and least promising of objects. His symbol is Van Gogh's *The Chair*.

This is not the chair of a Dutch still life, transformed by its surrounding objects and its lighting into an element of that atmosphere of quiet comfort to which the Netherlands in their decline made everything contribute. The chair is isolated—with no more than a hint of uneasy repose—standing as an ideogram of the very name Van Gogh. After smoldering so long, the latent conflict between the artist and the "outside world" had flared up at last.

The landscape was to become more and more unlike what had been termed a landscape in the past, for the earth would disappear from it; and a still life would bear less and less resemblance to what had always been considered a still life. Gone are the copper pots and pans and all the other objects brought to gleaming life by the reflection of light; in still lifes of today the glitter of Dutch glassware has given way to Picasso's packets of tobacco. A still life by Cézanne stands in the same relation to a Dutch still life as does a Cézanne figure to a Titian nude. If landscapes and still lifes—along with some nudes and depersonalized portraits, which are themselves still lifes—have come to rank as major *genres*, this is not because Cézanne was so fond of apples, but because there was more room for Cézanne in a painting of apples than there had been for Raphael in a portrait of Leo X.

I once heard one of our great modern painters remark to Modigliani: "You can paint a still life just as you wish, and the collector will be delighted; a landscape, and he will still be delighted; a nude, and he may begin to look worried; his wife—well, that depends ... But when you set to work to paint his own portrait, if you dare to tamper with his sacred mug, then, my friend, you will see him jump!" Even among those who genuinely appreciate painting there are many who fail, until confronted with their own faces, to understand this curious alchemy of the painter that makes their loss his gain. Every artist of the past who acted thus was modern in some sense; Rembrandt was the first great master whose sitters sometimes dreaded seeing their portraits. 65

◀ 40. *Van Gogh - The Chair and the Pipe*.

The only face with which a modern painter will sometimes "negotiate" is his own—and these self-portraits are often curiously suggestive.

The annexation of the model by the painter, of the world by painting, then took on a character without precedent, because, for the first time, the great artists no longer expressed, no longer recognized, the supreme value of the civilization in which they lived. This value, whether it was indeterminate or universally proclaimed, had been recognized by Michelangelo, Titian, Rubens, Poussin, even by Chardin, and by all the artists of the ages of faith. Rembrandt was at least a Christian painter, while Cézanne was a painter who went to Mass but *could not* paint a crucifix. But Western civilization (which was becoming a civilization of world conquest) was no longer animated by a supreme value. This fact was a basis for the conflict between Romanticism and the bourgeoisie; but Romanticism ended by singing the praises of progress, and its supreme value had been the sublime, which it expected would be revealed *by* the arts. There assuredly exists a supreme value for modern painters, but it is painting itself. The art of the end of the nineteenth century seems to us, quite legitimately, to be of an unprecedented individualism; but these individuals, when they painted (and as for Rodin's values they were not exclusively of a plastic nature), were all working in the service of the same value. For them, the future was not the time of progress but the time of posterity. For them, Courbet's romanticism and realism were not elements of a sermon; they were differing elements of the same palette. A palette linked with their own, allied against the common enemy: the ludicrous fiction admired by a ludicrous society, and deprived of any transcendent quality.

Precursors of an outcast art—and occasionally made to remember it— Rembrandt and Goya had not thought of solitude as a necessary condition of their vocation. It was solitude, in fact, that revealed his true vocation to Goya. In the nineteenth century a special kind of solitude, at once contemptuous and creative, soon came to seem the natural lot of the artist. François Villon considered himself a vagabond and perhaps a great poet as well, but not as a genius reduced to petty thievery by the injustices of the monarchy; and how can we picture his contemporary, Jean Fouquet, as an adversary of Louis XI? Michelangelo argued with the Pope, not with the papacy. Phidias was no more an enemy of Pericles, or a Sumerian sculptor of Prince Gudea, than was Titian of his Republic, of the Emperor Charles V or King Francis I. The break between the nineteenth-century artist and a tradition that had lasted four thousand years was no less brutal than that between the Machine Age and all the ages that preceded it. Artists no longer spoke to the public at large, or to any given class, but only to a group that was rigidly limited by its acceptance of their values.

Thus there now existed side by side not two schools but two distinct functions of painting. They came into being almost simultaneously, and from the same break with the past. If it should happen one day that our works of art are the sole survivors of a Europe blasted out of recognition and lost to memory, the historians of that future age will be led to assume that there existed in Paris, between 1870 and 1914, two antagonistic civilizations having no contact whatever with each other. On one side there was the pictorial world of Cormon, Bonnat, Bouguereau, and Roll; and on the other the world of Manet, Seurat, Van Gogh, and Cézanne. All of the artists—Rodin as well as Cézanne, Gustave Moreau as well as Degas—for whom painting was a supreme value were nauseated by this *Portrait of a Great Surgeon Operating*, by these *Greedy Kitchen Boys* and these *Cats in a Basket*, because they saw in them not just a tedious kind of painting but the absolute negation of painting. This antagonism had nothing to do with any traditional "conditioning" or training; many of the independents had studied in the same studios as their adversaries. Although they disliked middle-class values (their attitude toward politics was usually one of scornful detachment), they had no illusions about the proletarian who, on the rare occasions when he lingered before the window of a dealer in pictures, much preferred Bonnat to Degas. Here the sociologist should proceed cautiously; the *art* which followed that which had once been bought by the aristocracy was not one bought by the middle class; it was an art that no one bought.

Artists now began to gather their individual solitudes into a collective group. In the seventeenth century, all of the arts had centered on the same esthetic, but painters, poets, and musicians had little contact with each other. After the end of the eighteenth century, the arts diverged, but the artists drew closer together. And together they began their attack on the usurpation of values. It was not through his own art that Diderot had come in contact with painters, but through "philosophy." The poetry of the eighteenth century in no way coincided with the painting of the same period: what specific problem confronted in poetry by Delille or Dorat would have found an echo in a problem confronted in painting by Fragonard? But with the coming of Romanticism, painters, poets, and musicians joined together in their attempt to lay the foundations of that other-worldly universe they felt it was art's function to create. However diverse their various quests, all bore the stamp of the same refusal to co-operate with the society around them. Some years later, Wagner would write: "No man on whom a good fairy has not bestowed at birth the spirit of divine discontent with all existing things will ever discover anything new." Each artist brought back to the clan of friendly rivals the spoils of his victories, which, while they constantly broadened the rift between him and society, tended to anchor him ever more firmly in the closed society in which art was man's whole *raison d'être*. All of our great solitaries, from Baudelaire to Rimbaud, were also men who spent a good deal of their time in the literary cafés; even the rebellious Gauguin attended Mallarmé's Tuesday gatherings, and Mallarmé was a close friend of Manet, as Baudelaire had been of Delacroix. It was, in fact, not the theorists or critics, but the poets—Baudelaire and Mallarmé specifically—who possessed the surest instinct of the painting of their time. The vocabulary of the artists—not in their elaboration of theories, but in their notes, their conversation, their letters—often recalls the language of religious experience, revised and edited in slang.

The humanist styles had been one of the adornments of the civilization to which they belonged; the development of other styles that tended to make of art a restricted domain brought artists closer together in a ratio corresponding to their increasing separation from the traditional culture of their times. Racine, and even Sophocles, for that matter, were of little importance to painters obsessed with Velazquez, and soon to be obsessed by the Primitives. There had been no precedent, even in Florence, for a closed circle of artists of this kind, but art had now become a realm for which life furnished nothing more than the raw material. Within this realm, a man was judged only in terms of his ability to convey to others a world created by himself. Thus there came into being a sect of dedicated men, more determined to transmit their values than to impose them on others; conferring a sort of royal appointment on both its saints and its eccentrics; more gratified by its clandestine nature—like all sects—than its adherents would have admitted; and capable of sacrifice in the cause of its obscure and imperious truth. All of the characteristics of a sect were here, even that of renunciation.

Far more categorically than Delacroix, Manet and Cézanne made the statement that the tourist is a very different man from the pioneer and that one does not achieve equal status with those he admires by imitating their works. The great modern painters' appeal to posterity is linked to their ardent dialogue with those whom they held to be their masters. In their eyes, all true painting carried within itself its own posterity, since true painting was that element of painting which seems not to have been subordinated to spectacle—

that is, its indestructible element. Along with the history of painting and the discovery of its infinite diversity, artists were becoming immediately aware of a life after death of which the early Mediterranean forms of beauty seemed no longer anything more than a fugitive expression. With this knowledge came the ambition to recapture and perpetuate a language whose beginnings were lost in the mists of time.

In the service of this language, they accepted misery as part of life itself. From Baudelaire to Verlaine, from Daumier to Modigliani, the human sacrifice that was made! Rarely has so great a number of great artists offered so great a number of sacrifices to an unknown god. Unknown because those who served him, though vividly conscious of his greatness, could describe it only in their own language: painting. Even the artist most disdainful of the bourgeois (by which he meant the unbeliever), painting his most ambitious picture, would have felt uncomfortable had he been forced to use the vocabulary that expressed his ambition. No one spoke of truth, but everyone, confronted with the works of their adversaries, spoke of deception. What did the phrase "art for art's sake" imply that it should have caused Baudelaire to smile? Simply the picturesque. But no one smiled any longer when it began to be suspected that what was involved here was not a matter either of the picturesque or of beauty, but of a faculty that transcends time and restores dead works to life; and that the artist's faith, like all other faiths, was an attempt to seize and hold its own eternity. The outcast painter had taken his place in history; haunted from this point on by visions of his own absolute and confronted with an increasingly vulnerable humanism, the artist came to find in his very ostracism the source of an unexampled fertility. Having traced on the maps so many itineraries of misery, as if drawn in wavering trails of blood, these wretched studios where Van Gogh and Gauguin met were destined to flood the world with a glory equaling Leonardo's. Cézanne believed that his paintings would go to the Louvre, but not that reproductions of them would hang in every city in America; Van Gogh suspected that he was a great painter, but not that, fifty years after his death, he would be more famous in Japan than Raphael. This entire century that was so obsessed with cathedrals would leave only one behind it: the museum where its paintings would be gathered together.

This painting, which was held to be a supreme value in itself, does not make reference to any heritage: the unreal, the sacred, or the Christian faith. It also lays no claim to an imitation of nature, but in employing a theory of vision as a basis for its legitimacy, Impressionism limited pictorial discovery to personal interpretation and, as a result, reserved for nature the role of reference for art. *"To paint like Poussin, after nature ..."* Cézanne said; but if he means to compete with Poussin, it is of little importance to us that he does it after nature. We admire him not for his "little sensation," but for the creation of a rigid style worthy of that of the sculptors of Aegina, of the Tuscan painters of the first half of the fifteenth century, Masaccio or Piero della Francesca. Although the Impressionists had been able to consider their art more the expression of a vision than a style, the will to style reappeared at the end of the century with Cézanne, Gauguin, Seurat—and, in another realm, with Van Gogh.

And the museum without walls continues along the path of its metamorphosis.

Along with the new freedom of color, painters had discovered the Primitives—who were admired in Italy as pioneers—from Botticelli back to Giotto. Byzantium was not yet a factor of importance; but artists had also discovered Egypt, Mesopotamia, and Mexico, although in a more uncertain fashion. The sculpture of the ancient Orient, the painting of the Quattrocento, did not answer to the religious or emotional need for which Gothic art had provided an answer at the beginning of the century—no new *Génie du Christianisme* solicited their resurrection—they answered to an artistic need. It had been generally agreed that a picture had some claim to beauty when what it depicted, had it become real, would have been a thing of beauty; a theory which applied directly to Raphael and Poussin and, more subtly, even to Rembrandt. But what would an Assyrian bas-relief or an Aztec statue have meant if they were to come to life? Just what *Olympia* would mean if she were to come to life: nothing. Painting was no longer projecting itself into a world of the imaginary. Great forms of human self-expression were being discovered, free of any attempt at faithful imitation; it seemed apparent, therefore, that there existed a certain relationship between imitation and the ornament or the hieroglyph. With the revelation of the *Parcae* brought back from Greece by Lord Elgin, and of all those Greek statues whose emergence killed the contemporary myth of Hellas, as it killed their Roman copyists, it became apparent that Phidias bore no resemblance to Canova (it came as a bitter surprise to Canova to discover this for himself, in the British Museum); and in the meantime the pre-Columbian arts were beginning to be widely known. "I have in mind," Baudelaire wrote in 1860, "that streak of inevitable, synthetic, childlike savagery which is still perceptible in many a perfect type of art (Mexican, Ninevite, Egyptian, for instance), and which derives from the need to see things on a grand scale and to consider them chiefly as to their effect as a whole." Those styles that paralyzed their figures in a kind of hieratic transfiguration either insinuated or boldly stated that a system of organized forms dispensing with imitation can defy the natural scheme of things and, indeed, re-create the world.

True, Baroque also distorted the human figure, but flamboyant Baroque (with the exception of El Greco, who was regarded at the time by those who knew of him as more of a belated Gothic than a Baroque artist) belonged to a world of movement and emotion. But the ancient Orient had no more in common with this form of theater than does the most modern art. Although no one was unaware of what the austerity of the styles of the Nile and the Euphrates owed to their architecture, the museum gathered together only works that had been separated from the monuments to which they originally belonged; and the artist seldom deprecates, simply because of their origins, the forms that inspire him. Freed of their architecture and separated from their gods, these forms suggested that the work of art can affirm its implicit genius, not only by a harmonious accord of its parts, but also by a specific accord; and that, finally, art could submit the forms of life to the artist instead of submitting the artist to forms of life.

It was a suggestion that was still confused and incomplete. But it occurred at the same time as the first impact of Japanese prints. Everyone today is familiar with this impact, but we are often mistaken about its actual role because we take it to be the influence of a specific exoticism and script. When Van Gogh confessed the debt owed to the prints of Yamato by all of the independent painters—and primarily by himself—it was not because of his taste for mousmees or because of an admiration for arabesques. At a time when all two-dimensional art was considered clumsy (even Baudelaire speaks of naïveté), these prints revealed that such an art is compatible with supremely skillful drawing. Like the sketch, but with greater force because they are the expression of a deliberate art form (and they were aided by the element of their surprise), they in no way provided artists with models; they revealed to them their freedom.

A freedom that was also revealed to them by Byzantium, whose art, when it was finally rediscovered in Venice and Ravenna, inspired in Taine only the scorn expressed in his *Philosophy of Art*. These successive discoveries, along with that of medieval sculpture, which was to follow them (not precede them), resulted in the discovery that there exists in art a freedom which is by no means limited to personal interpretation. The Byzantine painter did

71

not see in the Byzantine style; he invented the Byzantine style, or translated what he saw into this style. To him, being an artist meant precisely to be capable of such creation or such translation. He made the elements he was depicting comply with the laws of a sacred universe: his tools, those of ceremony and those of ritual, became one. And the characteristics that distinguished Rembrandt, Velazquez, and Poussin—a realistic countenance or an idealized countenance—became matters of little circumstance in comparison with those that separate everything in a Sumerian statue or an Assyrian bas-relief, from Giotto perhaps, from Byzantium certainly. When confronted with the taut and massive styles of the ancient Orient, or with the rueful abstraction of Byzantium, all of the European schools represented in the Louvre—which the Avignon *Pietà* had not yet entered—become one single style.

Although the highest tradition of the museum was to remain for a time the dominant element in the history of art, at least it was no longer the whole history of art. That great tradition formed a compact *bloc*, isolated from the new territories that were being discovered on every side and opening vistas on an as yet uncharted world. The proper sphere of oil painting was becoming something that, more than any theory or even the dreams of the greatest artists, had brought together the pictures in the museums: not, as had been thought until now, a question of technique and a succession of methods of representation, but a language independent of the thing portrayed, and as specific as that of music. True, none of the great museum painters had been unaware that this language existed, but all had given it a subordinate place. What art was seeking, and what was found by Daumier's cautious and by Manet's sometimes agressive genius, was not a modification of the tradition, similar to the changes brought about by the work of earlier masters, but a break as profound as that which was now being brought about by the resurrection of long-forgotten styles. Another style, not another school.

It was at this point that the talents of painters ceased to be a means of expression for fiction.

Their talent. As for painting itself, well after the turn of the century anecdotes and heroic themes would continue to clutter the walls of the official Salons; painting would continue to depict a world of the imagination, but it would be the work of painters who no longer counted. Poetry shared in this adventure and was transformed in the same fashion; with Baudelaire it utterly discarded the story, even though official poetry continued to wallow for years in narrative and dramatic lyrics. The fact that Zola and Mallarmé

41. *Rubens - Abraham's Sacrifice.*

could be united in an admiration for Manet is less unexpected than it might seem: different, and sometimes contradictory as were their points of view, naturalism, symbolism, and modern painting combined to deal a deathblow to the vast empire of fiction, whose last expression was historic Romanticism.

But, after fifty years of comfortable and inglorious dying, the representation of fiction—and notably that of historic Romanticism—was to achieve a luxurious resurrection and find its true place : the cinema.

Once the era of discoveries in the technique of representation came to an end, painting followed the example of Rubens and began to cast feverishly

73

about for a means of rendering movement, as if movement alone could now impart that power of conviction which had once been implemented by each successive discovery. But possession of movement called for more than a change in methods of portrayal. The gestures that seemed to be those of

42. *Early Photography - La Castiglione.*    43. *Recent Photography - Dancer.*

drowning men and are common to the world of the Baroque do not represent a modification of the image; they are a succession of images. It is not surprising that an art so obsessed with theatrical effect, all gestures and emotion, should end with the motion picture.

The photograph had proved its usefulness for such necessities as passports. But in its attempt to represent life, photography, which evolved from Byzantine immobility to a frenzied Baroque in the space of thirty years, inevitably came up against all of the painter's old problems of representation. And where the painter had halted, it too was forced to halt. And was even further paralyzed by the fact that it had no scope for fiction; it could record a dancer's leap, but it could not show the Crusaders entering Jerusalem. But, from the faces of saints to the reconstruction of history, man's will to describe has always been focused as much on what he has never seen as on that with which he is familiar.

The four-centuries-old struggle to capture movement thus came to a halt at the same point in photography as it had in painting; and the cinema, even though it could record movement, merely substituted mobile for immobile gesticulation. If the great drive toward representation, which came to a standstill in Baroque, was to continue, the camera had to be made independent of the scene it was portraying. The problem was not solved mechanically, by a transformation of the camera, but artistically, by the invention of cutting.

When the motion picture was merely a device for showing figures in movement, it was no more an art than recording for the phonograph, or ordinary photography. Within a defined space, that of a real or imagined stage, actors performed a comedy or a drama, and the camera simply recorded their performance. The birth of the cinema as a means of expression dates from the abolition of that narrowly defined space; from the time when the producer first had the idea of recording a succession of brief shots instead of merely photographing a play; of sometimes moving the camera closer to the object so as to enlarge the figures on the screen, and sometimes moving it back; and, above all, of replacing the limitations of the theater by a wide field of vision, the area shown on the screen, into and from which the players made their entries and exits, and an area that the producer chose instead of having it imposed on him. The means of reproduction in the cinema is the moving photograph, but its means of expression is the sequence of planes. [1]

Legend has it that D. W. Griffith, when directing one of his early films, was so deeply moved by the expression of an actress at a certain moment of the filming that he had the cameraman take a series of shots of her, coming closer and closer each time, and then intercalated her face into the appropriate contexts. Thus the close-up was invented. The story illustrates the manner in which one of the great pioneers of film making applied his genius to its problems, seeking less to operate on the actor (by making him play differently, for instance) than to modify the relations between him and the spectator (by increasing the dimensions of his face). When this daring innovation of cutting a body at the waistline changed the whole course of the

[1] The planes change when the camera is moved; it is their sequence that constitutes cutting.

motion picture, commercial photographers, even the least advanced of them, had long given up the practice of photographing their sitters full length and were taking them half length, or concentrating on the faces. But as long as the camera and its field were static, the shooting of two characters half length would have necessitated making the entire film in this manner.

Thus the cinema acquired the status of an art only when the director, thanks to this use of different planes, was freed from the limitations of the theater. From this point on, he could choose the significant shots and coordinate them, making up for the silence of the medium by its selectivity. It would cease to be simply a photography of the theater and become the ideal medium for the expression of fiction.

When this occurred, fiction and pictorial talent had been separated for more than half a century. The cinema confirmed the separation and made any reconciliation impossible. The suggestion of movement, as it exists in the "captured images" of the Far East, of Degas, or in the snapshot; and, at the opposite end of the pole, the symbolization of movement, as we find it in the work of Uccello, in the bas-reliefs of the ancient Orient, or in the abstractions of Scythian art, had taken the place once held in the plastic arts by the representation of movement. The rivalry between artistic creation and the fiction on which official art still lived had lost all meaning. Representational values, which once had been the dominant characteristic of painted fiction, were swallowed up in a world rediscovered by the cinema and apparently universal: a desire to seduce and to move, the style and poetry of the theater, the cult of beauty in individuals, of emotion in countenances. In the depth of centuries past, a ritual mask solemnly chants and dances in the firelight; before our eyes today, the distorted faces of close-ups whisper through the shadows they define and fill.

But, once illusion had ceased to be the privileged domain of expression, sacred sculpture and two-dimensional painting assumed their real importance. Although no one yet realized it, it was the beginning of a process of leveling-off for all the painting of the world. Egypt, Mesopotamia, Greece, Rome, Mexico, Persia, India, China, Japan—two-dimensional painting is that of the entire world, with the exception of a period of a few centuries in the West. Responding to this vast effort of creation, and at the same time encouraging it, reproduction was on the threshold of distributing to the world, for the first time, the forms that artists of every nation have resurrected, admired, foreseen, or ignored.

Photography, which at first was an unpretentious means of making known acknowledged masterpieces to those who could not buy engravings, seemed destined merely to perpetuate established values. But at present an ever-greater range of works is being reproduced, in ever greater numbers, while the technical conditions of reproduction are influencing the choice of the works selected. Moreover, their distribution is sustained by a commercial approach of constantly increasing subtlety and extent. It often substitutes the significant work for the obvious masterpiece, and the pleasure of learning for that of simply admiring. An earlier generation was content with engravings of Michelangelo; today, we photograph the works of lesser masters, folk paintings, and arts that once were unknown. In fact, everything that can be considered in terms of a style is now being photographed.

For while photography was bringing a profusion of masterpieces to the artists, the artists themselves were revising their attitude toward the very concept of a masterpiece.

From the sixteenth to the nineteenth century, the masterpiece was a work that existed in itself. An all-powerful esthetic had established an ideal of beauty based on what was thought to be the legacy of Greece. The work of art constantly aspired toward this ideal representation: in Raphael's time, a masterpiece was a painting on which the imagination could not possibly improve. There was little question even of comparing it with other works of the same artist. It held no place as a work of its time, but only as an element in the rivalry—to which all else was considered subordinate—with the ideal work it suggested. Rubens, who became the symbol of a power of color actually discovered *in Venice*, freed official painting from Italian idealization only to submit it to an opulent transformation that in turn was willingly accepted by the Italians: the heroine of his greatest *ensemble* of paintings is a daughter of the Medici.

In the period between the Roman sixteenth and the European nineteenth centuries, this esthetic lost much of its original strength, but until the advent of Romanticism it was generally conceded that the truly great work of art carried its genius within itself. History and antecedents counted for nothing; its success constituted its identification. This Arcadian conception, which rejected, with a firmness as uninformed as it was unconscious, the determina-

77

tion of each century to discover its own genius, came under attack simultaneously with the dawning awareness of different conceptions of art whose distant and secret kinship was unconsciously recognized, even though their connecting link remained unknown.

Until the minor paintings of the royal collections were first exhibited in 1750 it was doubtless the shops of the picture dealers—which themselves figure in so many canvases, even so late as *L'Enseigne de Gersaint*—that had made it possible for artists to see varying arts side by side. But they were almost always minor works, and subservient to an esthetic as yet unchallenged. In 1710, Louis XIV owned 1299 French and Italian pictures and 171 "of other schools." With the exception of Rembrandt—who impressed Diderot for such curious reasons ("If I saw in the street a man who had stepped out of a Rembrandt canvas, I would want to follow him, admiringly; if I saw one out of a Raphael, I suspect I would have to be tapped on the shoulder before I even noticed him.")—and with the exception, especially, of the most Italian of Rubens' work, the eighteenth century could see, outside of Italy, nothing but minor paintings. Who then, in 1750, would have considered comparing Jan van Eyck with Guido Reni? Italian painting and antique sculpture were the highest achievements of a civilization that still reigned supreme in the imagination. In the royal galleries, Italy was queen. Neither Watteau nor Fragonard nor Chardin wanted to paint like Raphael; but no one thought of proclaiming them his equals. There had been a "Golden Age" of art.

When the Louvre became a museum, after the Revolution, and what had been the royal collections were augmented by the conquests of Napoleon, the various schools of art at last confronted each other with their varying masterpieces, but the traditional esthetic remained supreme. What was not Italian was evaluated, as a matter of course, in terms of its Italian content. It was only by speaking Italian that an artist gained admission to the Academy of the Immortals, even if he spoke it with Rubens' accent. In the eyes of critics of the period a masterpiece was a canvas that "held its own" in the company of the acknowledged masterpieces of the Salon Carré: Rembrandt, a magnificent, disturbing figure, was relegated to the outskirts; Velazquez and Rubens were accepted only because of an "agreement" with the Venetian school of the Italian hierarchy. It was an agreement the true countenance of which was to be clearly revealed before the death of Delacroix: academicism. Thus a rivalry of the canvases themselves replaced their former rivalry with a mythical perfection. But in this "debate with the illustrious dead," in which every new masterpiece was called on to state its claim to rank with a privileged élite, the test of merit, even when Italian supremacy was on the wane, was still the common measure of the qualities that those time-honored works possessed. It was a measure determined by the three-dimensional oil paintings of the sixteenth and seventeenth centuries; a debate in which the sketches of Delacroix had little place, in which Manet would have no place at all.

Photographic reproduction was to aid in changing the tenor of this debate by suggesting, then imposing, a new hierarchy.

Whether Rubens was admired because some of his least Flemish canvases were considered equal to Titian becomes a matter of secondary importance when placed in the context of an album containing Rubens' entire work. Such an album is a world in itself. In it *The Arrival of Marie de Medici* invites comparison with Rubens' other works far more than it does with

44. *Rubens - Landscape with a Cart.*

Titian or with Raphael; and primarily with the sketch from which the finished painting was made. *The Portrait of a Child* in the Liechtenstein Gallery, the *Atalanta*, the *Philopoemen*, the *Landscape with a Cart* take on a wholly new accent here. And we discover that Rubens was one of the greatest landscape painters in the world. The true anthology begins. The truly great work of art is no longer the one most perfectly in accord with a tradition—no matter how liberal that tradition may be—nor is it the most complete, the most "finished" work; it is the one in which the artist, *in relation only to himself*, has touched the pinnacle of his style and stripped away everything that is not uniquely his own: the most significant work of the inventor of a style. In one sense, the private exhibition—the "one-man show"—which was unknown to earlier generations, thus isolates the painter: the great romantic artists used to exhibit at the Salons, to which our great contemporaries send their canvases only as a friendly gesture. Just as, at one time, the masterpiece that conquered the imagination, and later the masterpiece that was accepted into the company of the immortals, was joined and sometimes replaced by the most telling work of the artist in question, so now another class of work is coming to the fore: the most significant or accomplished work of every style. An album of Oceanian art, by familiarizing us with two hundred works of sculpture, also reveals to us the quality of some among them; any assemblage of a large number of works of the same style creates the masterpieces of that style because it compels us to an understanding of its essential intent and its particular meaning. The album, like the exhibition, renders impossible any comparison of the Oceanian or African mask with a "model," with the heads of classic statuary, and even, for that matter, with those of Romanesque statues; the mask must here be compared only with its fellows—to whatever civilization they may belong, but primarily with its own.

The revision of values on the nature of art that began in the nineteenth century, the end of the imperative esthetic, did away with the prejudice against clumsiness. The disdain for Gothic art that prevailed in the seventeenth century was due, not to any authentic conflict of values, but to the fact that the Gothic statue was regarded at that time, not as what it really is, but as a failure to be *something else:* it was assumed that the Gothic sculptor had intended to carve a classic statue, and if he had not achieved it, it was because *he had not known how to*. The singular notion that, in the Middle Ages, antique sculpture had become inimitable or had disappeared (when, in fact, copies of the antique were being made in the South of France in the eleventh century, and it had required only a command from Frederick II of Hohenstaufen for Roman art to reappear—to say nothing of the fact that Italian artists walked past Trajan's column every day) was generally accepted because idealization had demanded a new series of discoveries in the art of representation, and no one imagined that these were a matter of indifference to the Gothic artists. Louis XIV's exclamation: "Away with those monstrosities!" included Notre Dame. The same attitude, carried over to the beginning of the nineteenth century, caused the canvas of *L'Enseigne de Gersaint* to be cut in two, and enabled the Goncourts to pick up their Fragonards in junk shops. A dead style is one that is defined solely by what it is not.

Isolated works of an imperfectly known style, unless it should come into sudden prominence as a precursor (as Negro art came into prominence because of Picasso), almost always provoke "negative" reactions. For how many centuries has not this same Negro art been regarded as the work of sculptors who knew nothing of their craft? And—like fetishes and masks— the Greek archaics, the sculpture of the Nile and the Euphrates were *widely scattered* when they first became a part of our culture. Single works, groups of works, even cathedral statuary, were thus forced to *insinuate themselves* into the artistic consciousness that had discovered them, into a company of masterpieces more coherent, more unyielding, and vaster even than that of literary masterpieces: Théophile Gautier disdained Racine on the strength of Victor Hugo, and perhaps Poussin on the strength of Delacroix; but not Michelangelo, or even Raphael. A great Egyptian work of art was originally admired in proportion to its accordance, however subtle this might be, with the Mediterranean tradition; we admire it in proportion to its independence of that tradition.

Traditional works were compared, classified, and reproduced, while the others were relegated to an obscurity from which only a few emerged, as fortunate exceptions or as examples of an alleged decadence. It is this that accounts for the readiness of the connoisseur of the period to recognize this decadence as such, and to define it primarily in terms of what is missing from it. A portfolio of Baroque art constitutes a rehabilitation since it separates the Baroque from its relationship to the classical, and makes of it something other than just a voluptuous and disordered classicism.

Moreover, much as Gothic seems to have been led toward classical art by a series of gradations, a similar process, in reverse, led to the rediscovery of Gothic art: Romanticism had rediscovered the picturesque, dreamlike quality of Notre-Dame de Paris, but not the austere spirituality of Romanesque. In art every resurrection has a way of beginning step by step. Reproduction, because of the mass of works it sets before us, frees us from the necessity of this tentative approach; by revealing a style in its entirety—just as it displays an artist's work in its entirety—it forces each to rely on its basic significance.

45. *Early Photography - The Lady of Elche*.

And since reproduction, though not the cause of our intellectualization of art, is its most effective tool, the craft which is applied to it, aided sometimes by chance, carries this intellectualization constantly forward.

The angle from which a work of sculpture is photographed, the manner in which it is framed and centered, and, above all, a *carefully studied* lighting—the lighting of some famous works is beginning to share a degree of attention that once was granted only to film stars—may strongly accentuate something that previously had been only suggested.

In addition to this, black and white photography imparts a family likeness

82

46. *Recent Photography - The Lady of Elche (detail)*. ▶

to objects that have actually but slight affinity. When reproduced on the same page, such widely differing objects as a tapestry, an illuminated manuscript, a painting, a statue, or a medieval stained-glass window lose their colors, their texture, and dimensions (the sculpture also loses something of its volume), and it is their common style that benefits.

47. *Mesopotamian Art ( ?) - Goddess of Fertility.*

The development of reproduction has had another, more subtle consequence. In an album or an art book, objects are generally reproduced in more or less the same format; the limitations of the printed page are such that a reclining Buddha over sixty feet in length may appear to be about four times the size of a Tanagra figurine. The works reproduced lose *their relative proportions.*

It is of no importance that a large statue should become small: it simply becomes a commonplace document, and we are unlikely to make a mistake about its true nature. But the enlargement of seals, of coins, of amulets, of

48. *Goddess of Fertility (detail).*  ▶

figurines creates truly *fictitious arts*. The unfinished quality of the execution, resulting from the very small scale of these objects, now becomes a style, free and modern in its accent. The dialogue of our sculptors with the arts of

49. *Steatopygic Woman.*          50. *Female Musician.*

Mesopotamia gives birth to those strange figures suggested by photographs of cylinder seals or of Sumerian *Fertilities*. Undoubtedly, these photographs bring no more than a passing moment of glory to the works they represent, but the model becomes the basic material of an image rather than the image being a reproduction of the model. The historian (annoyed) cannot entirely neglect systems of forms that are a part of history and occasionally shed light on it; the artist (gratified) is conscious of the dialogue between one or another of the *Fertilities* and a particular sculpture of Picasso,

51. *Female Musician.*▶

between a certain Etruscan stone carving and a particular print of Braque.

The consequence of this "creation through photography" is sometimes incidental and sometimes considerable.

52. *Gallic Coin of the Osismii.*

Incidentally, it reveals some singular works, existing, as it were, on the borders of the civilization that created them. Lost in museums or in private collections, they were considered curiosities. Isolated and studied, they become interrogations, and when no place can be found for them in history they suggest great styles that have disappeared, or which "might have been." *The Musician* would disturb us less if her home were not in the Cairo museum.

But the role of reproduction becomes one of considerably altered importance when it touches on the minor arts. Certain of these, such as the pre-Buddhist terra cottas of Japan and Sardinian bronzes have no corresponding

53. *Japanese Art - Funerary Statuette Portraying a Monkey.* ▶

54. *Byzantine Art - Satyr and Maenad Dancing.*

55. *Mycenean Art - Goddess Enthroned.* ▶

56. *Etruscan Art - Aphrodite (?).*
57. *Colombian Art - Votive Figurine.*
58. *Sardinian Art - Warrior.*
59. *Etruscan Art - Engraved Mirror.*

major art. The majority of the others—Mycenaean ivories and those of earliest antiquity, some Etruscan bronzes, Gallic coins, the jewelry of the Andes,

60. *Egyptian Art - Woman Servant Milling Grain.*

African gold weights—possess only an uncertain relationship to their major arts: they complement them to a greater extent than they imitate them. It is difficult to imagine a study of Gallic art that would not include its coins; and to our artists this art is primarily one of these coins.

And, finally, enlargement makes some art forms, which for centuries have been studied and considered as minor arts, into rivals of their major arts. No Greek terra cotta moves us to the same degree as does the Koré of the Acropolis Museum, but photographs of a great many late terra cottas that have retained its austere style move us more than almost all of the statues that are their contemporaries. The basic material unquestionably plays its part in the style—or, rather, in the individual stamp—of these small objects; but perhaps it is more a matter of function than of material. Greek figurines, like those of the Chinese, come from tombs. But their funerary art is in no

94

61. *Greek Art (Aegestratos) - Aphrodite.* ▶

way funereal; we owe to it, in fact, the depiction of family life, more plebeian in Greece, more formal in China. The modeler of these figures, like the illustrator of vases, takes liberties with the people he is portraying that he could not accord himself in making a divine image.

62. *Greek Art - Seated Man Writing.*

63. *Greek Art - Lecythus (detail).* ▶

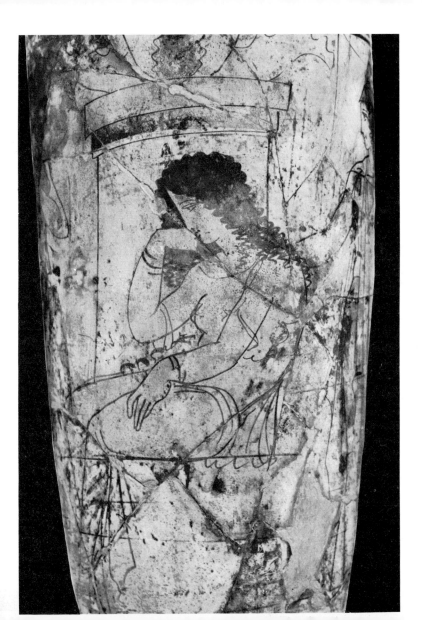

65. *Pala - Virgin in Majesty.*     66. *Pala - Evangelist ( ?).*

This liberty is evident in works of widely varying techniques. The ivories of the ancient Orient, the jades, the objects of gold and bronze have assumed a place in the museum without walls different from that of the treasures of not so long ago. The best known of Phoenician works is an ivory, one of the most beautiful of Cretan works is in gold: the Vaphio cup. Photographs of ivories and of gold and silverware are indispensable to any study of Christian artistic expression. We know of no Byzantine bas-relief that can be likened to the *Triumphant Emperor* in Trier, no major stone sculpture similar to the working of the bronze doors that cover the face of Europe from Verona to Novgorod. Enlargements reveal to us, not only in the ivories, but in all of Christian expression in precious metals—even the Gothic—a dramatic accent different from that of monumental sculpture or of sculpture in wood.

◀ 64. *Reliquary of St. Maurice d'Agaune (detail).*

67. *Annunciation of the Angel to Joseph* (12th century).

68. *Byzantine Art - Barberini Ivory.* ▶

69. *Assyrian Art - Ashurnasirpal Hunting the Lion (detail)*.

The specific life which is given to a work by an enlargement of it attains
its greatest strength in the dialogue permitted—indeed, demanded—by a
comparison of photographs. The art of the Steppes was a highly specialized
form, but if its bronze or gold plaques are shown beside a bas-relief, in the

same format, they themselves become bas-reliefs, as do the seals of the ancient Orient, from Crete to the Indus. Thus reproduction frees their style from the limitations that made it seem a minor art.

It goes even further in freeing works of a less marginal nature whose greatness of style makes them the equal of others far better known. In the

70. *Iranian Art - Cylinder Seal.*

metopes of Selinus, the museum without walls has shown us the rivals to the pediments of the Parthenon. And we may be sure that Romanesque sculpture would seem to us less rich and less complex if the museum did not give cornices the breadth of a lintel and the accent of a tympanum—just as it gives to so many ivories the dignity of a bas-relief.

In the school of fictitious arts, the fragment is one of the great masters. Does not the *Victory of Samothrace* suggest a Greek style divergent from the true Greek style? In Khmer statuary there were many admirable heads on conventional bodies; those heads, removed from the bodies, are now the pride of the Musée Guimet. The body of the *St. John the Baptist* in the Rheims porch is far from bearing out the genius of the isolated head. Enhanced by the manner in which it is presented, and appropriately lit, a fragment makes possible a reproduction which is not one of the least worthy inhabitants of the museum without walls. To this fact we owe the many albums of Primitive    103

71. *Romanesque Art - Vézelay - Pentecostal Christ (detail).* ▶

72. *Byzantine Art - Christ Crowning the Emperor Roman II and the Empress Eudoxia.* ▶

landscapes derived from details of miniatures and pictures; Greek vase paintings displayed as if they were frescoes; and the general use in modern monographs of the expressive detail. We can study Gothic figures separated from the profusion of the cathedrals, and Indian art freed of the luxuriance of its temples but retaining their atmosphere. The isolation of the album some-

73. *Gothic Art (Rheims) - St. John the Baptist.*

times brings about a metamorphosis resulting from enlargement, sometimes enables us to discover and compare, and sometimes reveals facts we had not previously known. Through his use of the fragment, the photographer instinctively restores to certain works their due place in the company of the elect—just as the works contained in the museum of the past gained entrance through their quality of Italianism.

For it is also true that certain coins, certain objects, even certain recognized works of art have undergone a curious change and become subjects for admirable photographs. In much the same way that many ancient works owe the strong effect they make on us to an element of mutilation in what was clearly intended to be a perfect whole, so, when photographed with a special lighting, composition and stress on certain details, ancient works

74. *St. John the Baptist (detail).* ▶

75. *Gothic Art (Bamberg) - Eve (detail).*

76. *Gothic Art (Bamberg) - Adam (detail).*

of sculpture often acquire a quite startling, if spurious, modernism. Classical esthetic proceeded from the part to the whole; ours, often proceeding from the whole to the fragment, finds a precious ally in photographic reproduction.

An ally which is becoming better equipped with each passing day. Before 1950, book publishers could reproduce photographs of works of art, but not reproductions of these photographs: an American publisher, in order to reproduce the Giant Buddha of Lung-Men, which had often appeared in French and Japanese books, was forced to obtain the original photograph. The discovery of new processes of printing, by permitting black and white reproduction of *all other* reproductions, has substituted a universal library for individual collections of photographs.

Thus, there has come into being a world of sculpture far different from that of the museum. More complex, because it ranges from curiosities to master-pieces, from figurines to colossi; more far-reaching, because it covers the entire earth; of another nature, because it escapes the cemetery of museum galleries in which statues are assembled. The museum without walls cannot restore to these statues the temple, the palace, the church, or the garden they have lost; but it does deliver them from Necropolis. Because it isolates them; and especially—we must return to this again—because of the manner in which it lights them. No photograph of the *Victory of Samothrace* moves us as greatly as this isolated statue, crowning the high stairway of the Louvre on her prow of stone; but how many works of sculpture move us less than photographs of them, and how many have been revealed to us by photographs? The point has been reached where the real museum is beginning to resemble the museum without walls: its statues are better lit and far less frequently clustered together. Michelangelo's *Rondanini Pietà* in the Castello Sforzesco in Milan (it too is isolated) seems admirably posed, awaiting the photographers. It belongs to both the real world of statues and to an unreal world that extends its boundaries, just as the face of a very beautiful film star belongs to both the real world of feminine beauty and to an unreal world that exists only through photography. Photographs of sculpture in color will undoubtedly supplant photographs in black and white only when they have discovered the secret of that unreality; and perhaps at that time the world of the first museum without walls will rejoin that of the silent film—but films in color have not destroyed films in black and white. Even then, the isolation of the statues, the dialogue with their fellows imposed on them by lighting, the presence of all of the world's sculpture will continue to maintain a world of art without precedent; and every passing year brings further proof that it is not only a world of reproductions.

Photography of paintings has played a less complex role. Just as engravings once did, it has extended our understanding more than it has aroused our admiration, increased our knowledge, or stimulated our curiosity, since many of these photographs have played the part of ambassadors, standing in until the development of new processes of color reproduction.

These are still far from perfect, and can never do justice to an original of large dimensions. Still, there has been amazing progress in the last twenty years. The color reproduction does not compete with the actual masterpiece, it merely evokes it, or suggests it. But to reject it because of its weaknesses is as futile as it was, some years ago, to reject the phonograph record. It no more causes us to neglect the originals than the phonograph caused neglect of the concert hall. *It leads us to study those which are accessible to us, not to forget them;* and if they are inaccessible, what would we know of them without it?

For the past hundred years (if we except the activities of specialists), the history of art has been the history of that which can be photographed. Every man of culture is aware of the inevitability with which the course of Western sculpture, from Romanesque to Gothic, and from Gothic to Baroque, has led sculptors toward the expression of movement; but is he also aware of the parallel evolution of the stained-glass window, or of the drastic transformations that took place in Byzantine painting? The reason why the impression that Byzantine art was repetitive and static prevailed so long is, simply, that its drawing was bound up with a convention, while its true genius was recorded in its color. Formerly, years of research, ranging from Greek to Syrian monasteries, from museums to private collections, from picture sales to antique shops (and therewith a prodigious memory for color) were needed for a knowledge of Byzantine painting. Thus, until recently, its history was the history of its drawing. But in the history of art, drawing is going to lose the supremacy, once threatened at Venice, and then regained with the advent of black and white photography, which so often transformed Titian into a genius of tapestry design. A reproduction used to be thought all the more effective because the color was subordinated to the drawing. But, in the future, Chardin will no longer be disarmed in his combat with Michelangelo.

The problems peculiar to color are at last being asked and answered: the intrusion of tones of gray into paintings is perhaps no less significant than the birth of the arabesque. If we have made less of a study of styles of color than of styles of forms, it is because color reproduction was uncertain and diffi-

cult. Certain Italian mannerists, Il Rosso for example, and a whole school of the Spanish Baroque, brought about a radical change in the palette, a troubled harmony of yellows and violets of which a black and white photograph conveys nothing, and on which their whole art is founded. Since the time of the first edition of this book—thus, in less than fifteen years—the world's painting has rejoined its sculpture in our libraries. The multitude of *Virgins* known to everyone is now confronted with the army of Romanesque frescoes which were unknown to anyone except art historians before the First World War; with the world of the miniature, of tapestry, and, above all, of the stained-glass window; and with the discovery that color is not always, not necessarily, the exclusive prerogative of painting.

Like the enlargement of small works of sculpture, the enlargement of miniatures is giving them (and gave them, even in black and white) a wholly new importance, and relating them to larger works reduced in size for reproduc-

78. *The Book of the Love-stricken Heart - The Heart of the King.*

◀ 77. *Il Rosso - Love Chastised by Venus (detail).*

79. *Pol de Limbourg - Les Très Riches Heures du Duc de Berry.*

tion. We discovered them, as we have discovered so much else, by "going back in time": those of the fifteenth century, the Gothic, the Romanesque, those of the High Middle Ages, and those of Asia. Surely the master of *The Love-Stricken Heart* can claim a place in our museum without walls. The *Très Riches Heures du Duc de Berry* become cousins to Flemish painting, to the Broederlam triptych, yet without resembling them. Moreover, such subjects as the Limbourgs, Van Eyck, and Fouquet employed for their miniatures were those they had not, would not, have employed for paintings. If we want to know what landscape meant to a Northern artist in the year 1420, how can we neglect Pol de Limbourg? Certain works of this kind, when isolated by reproduction, suggest sometimes a great art, sometimes a vanished school (a thought which gives food for the imagination). In certain works by the

114

80. *The Master of the Heures de Rohan - Death Before His Judge.* ▶

81. *Ebbo Gospel Book (9th century) - Saint Mark.*

82. *Romanesque Art (Tavant) - The Virgin.* ▶

master of the *Heures de Rohan* we glimpse a precursor of Grünewald; given back its colors, the *Gospel Book* of Archbishop Ebbo of Rheims shows no less originality than the frescoes of Montoire and Tavant.

The miniature often remains a minor *genre* because of its character of an

85. *Siyah Kalem - Battle of a Hero and a Demon.*

applied art, or because of its dependence on conventions. The nineteenth century was already aware of the Gothic miniature and of the arabesques of Iran. But what of the illuminated manuscripts of Ireland and of Aquitaine; the Carolingian illuminations of every monastery and convent from the Rhine to the Ebro; the Byzantine style of Arab miniatures, the Turkish Album of Mehmed II, the Conqueror? And those miniatures in which a master has *invented* a personal style and not merely transposed pictures or imitated previous miniatures? The "civilization of the book," which was that of the convents and monasteries of the High Middle Ages, produced many more irrational forms than Gothic Christianity—and our contemporary artists are very rational in their discovery of irrational forms. Before another fifty years have passed, the works of prime importance will have been rescued from the jungle of illustrated manuscripts. Then the world will have discov-

◀ 83. *Bible of Saint-Aubin d'Angers - Christ in Majesty (detail).*
◀ 84. *Romanesque Art (Montoire) - Christ in Majesty (detail).*
86. *The Book of Kells (8th century) - Madonna and Child.* ▶

ered the link that binds the creation of sacred forms to the calligraphy of holy books, notably in Irish illuminations; just as another link binds the Chinese wash drawings of landscapes to the calligraphy of poems. Will our successors then remember that it was the exhibitions of pre-Romanesque illuminations in some of Europe's great libraries (primarily the French Bibliothèque Nationale) that first made known the painting of the "centuries without painting"? And will they be aware that, in adding to the traditional dialogue between the greatest sculptors of Christianity and the powerfully elemental sculpture of the eleventh century, their unknown dialogue with the forms so masterfully executed for the treasures of monasteries *before the year* 1000, these exhibitions have raised new questions concerning the very nature of Romanesque genius?

87. *Romanesque Art (Saint-Benoît-sur-Loire) - Capital (detail).*
88. *The Pontifical of Winchester (10th century) - Pentecost.*

89. *Delos - Dionysius Riding a Panther.*

Ancient mosaics, even some works of the very early epochs, are represented in our museums; but not Christian mosaics, which were unknown to the
royal collections and the museums of the nineteenth century. Like the sculp-

90. *Piazza Armerina - Africa.*

ture of the cathedrals, they make us conscious of the unexpected link established by the museum without walls between the fragment it brings to us—"released" by photography—and the totality of the sacred place. In the memory, the mosaic is a succession of scenes, perhaps simply of details or fragments, observed in reproduction, or at Monreale, Palermo, or Ravenna—for most of us, in the church of San Marco in Venice. An art which may yet be destined for the museum, but which, like that of stained glass, cannot enter into it without first undergoing an obvious metamorphosis. Because it seems more a handicraft than an art? It did seem so at a time when it was still looked on with disdain. It claims our attention because it is a sacred art *par excellence*. When it is no longer this or not yet this, it ceases to interest us: the mosaic in San Marco done from a design by Titian is irritating; our interest in the majority of Roman mosaics is not of the same nature as that we feel for the *Christ Pantocrator* of Monreale. It is, in fact, in all of the areas where Roman art was on the wane—Africa, Sicily, the East—that our interest is awakened. What vague presentiment of Byzantium imposed on the ancient mind this starkness, this new simplification, which sometimes appears hieratic and sometimes simply awkward; this refusal to imitate painting, which resulted in the abandonment of minute particles of stone and the use of larger ones (just as, centuries later, the unapparent brushwork of the Primitives would be abandoned for the visible brushwork of Venice), and which led the mosaic from portrayal of doves and comic characters—even from *The Battle of Arbela*—to the raw independence of North Africa, to the angular

125

*Seasons* of Antioch? The abandonment of ancient attempts at an illusion of relief stimulated the change in palette which brings the mosaic into that part of the museum without walls whose works are the direct ancestors of those of our own artists: the autocracy of color almost invariably follows the decline of illusionism. Whatever the dates of the Piazza Armerina mosaics, and the

91. *Piazza Armerina - The Great Hunt (detail).*

speculations historians indulge in concerning their girls in bikinis, the vaguely pre-Carolingian hunting scenes of the principal panels are imbued with a rose and gray harmony that can be likened to that of the temple of Palmyra, perhaps to certain of the Eastern Hellenistic harmonies, but not to those of Rome; and this is why we are so receptive to this art. In Santa Maria Maggiore, as in the first mosaics of Salonika, the song of color no longer owes anything to what Rome had inherited from Greece, and the break between an art of representation and what Braque called an art of presentation is not without analogy to the rupture between our last traditional art and our modern art. The Christian mosaic, an art destined for sanctuaries, was to disdain the imitation of appearance, and, placing autocracy of form and lyricism of color in the service of the world of God, would bring forth one of the most highly disciplined of all arts—an art our painters were to discover as an example of arbitrariness and of liberty.

126

92. *Doura-Europos - Two Adolescents of the Conon Family.* ▶

The nineteenth century considered the medieval stained-glass window an ornamental art. But here we must bear in mind that the realm of a decora-

tive art is precisely determinable only in an art of humanists. An ornamental casket of the seventeenth century clearly belongs in this realm, but does a reliquary? A Luristan bronze, a Scythian plaque, a Coptic fabric, certain Chinese animal figures—even a tapestry? One element of the reliquary is subordinated to the object it adorns? Less, no doubt, than a statue-column to the church of which it is a part; and the influence of the goldsmith's art on Romanesque stone sculpture is no longer questioned. It was by humanist criteria that the stained-glass window came to be defined in terms of what it was not, in much the same way as the seventeenth century judged Gothic sculpture. The stained-glass window is linked to a subordinate design, which is sometimes ornamental (though even here it must be studied at close

129

hand), but its color is in no sense an ornamental tinting of this design, a brilliant filling-in of space; it is a lyric expression, not without analogy to the pictorial lyricism of Grünewald or of Van Gogh. If the chromatic genius of Northern Europe appeared so late on the scene, it was because, for the great colorist, stained glass was the most powerful of its means of expression. And at the end of the nineteenth century our color-obsessed masters seemed to be calling forth a window to which *Père Tanguy* and *The Sunflowers* would be more closely related than they are to Titian or Velazquez. The very word "painting," born of pictures, misleads us: the high point of Western color, in the age before Giotto, is neither a fresco, nor a miniature; it is *Notre-Dame de la Belle Verrière* in the cathedral at Chartres. The art of the stained glass window *is*, of course, decorative, just as all of Romanesque art, even the statuary, is decorative. More often than not, this statuary would remain concealed beneath the enormous ornamental mass that hems it in, were it not for the human face that wrests it free. The robe of the statue-column is an element of the portal itself; the head is not. The stained-glass window of the twelfth, even of the thirteenth century, emerges whole from its setting of stone with the same force that liberates the Romanesque face; but even though, with the help of photography, each of us can instinctively isolate the statues of the Royal Portal of Chartres, it is still difficult for us to detach the stained-glass window from a confusion in which *Notre-Dame de la Belle Verrière* forms but a part of an elaborate lacework design. The liberating accent granted to sculpture by the face is bestowed on the window by a lyric expression as specific as that of music—an expression no artist can fail to recognize if he will but compare it with the other forms of Romanesque plastic art: the fresco or the mosaic. (And even its design is less Byzantine than it might appear.) We need only consider the great Romanesque windows as part of the company of frescoes, and of earlier or contemporary mosaics, to see that they form, not the background, but the fulfillment.

The stained-glass window is, most certainly, a monumental painting; in its foremost achievements no other can be compared with it: no fresco achieves so perfect a harmony with its architecture as does the window with Gothic architecture. The experience of war, when the windows were taken down and clear glass panes took their place, taught us at once that stained glass was a great deal more than mere ornamentation. Indifferent to the timeless age of what it represents, it is not so to the varying light of day, which gave it, as the hours passed and the faithful came and went, a vitality unknown to any other form of art. It replaced the dark golden field of the

130

mosaic as the free light of day replaced the somber lanterns of the crypts, and throughout the centuries the silent orchestra of the windows of Chartres has seemed to obey the baton held by the angel above the great sun dial.

Perhaps, with the help of photography, the sun may soon resume its role in the Gothic play of which it was once director-in-chief. We will go to see the portals of Chartres at the times best suited to the statues, so that we may observe them under different lights; and to see the windows, first when the sun passes through them and then when it lights the opposite face of the cathedral. (Reader, carry your field glasses, which by isolating the smaller scenes bring them to vivid life. We will discover that a great stained-glass window is as constantly changing as a landscape.

The genius of the stained-glass window ceases when the smile begins. Then drawing becomes paramount, and imitation (the personages painted by Giotto were "alive" to his contemporaries, just as Van Eyck's faces were true to life for his) becomes a value. Romanesque means of expression were those of the sacred. In the angular hierarchism of the great windows, akin to that of the great tympana, the eternal East had at last found its lyric expression: the stained-glass window was a mosaic given its place in the sun, and the rigid Byzantine trunk, nourished by barbarian migrations, came to full flower in the branches of the *Tree of Jesse*. This window did not provide a setting for the world of God, it was the expression of it, to the same extent as was the tympanum of Moissac, where a stunned assembly of ruffians, transformed by their crowns into Elders of the Apocalypse, contemplated the eternal in the form of a Christ in Majesty. But the vineyard workers carved in stone atop the columns of Burgundy, and painted in glass in the windows of Chartres, were to take the place of the Elders of Moissac; in Amiens, blacksmiths beat swords into ploughshares. And after this, the lyric outburst was to lose the accent it shared with the mosaic and the Romanesque tympana; the sacred forms in the tall windows of Chartres and of Bourges were to be replaced by the host of little people who shared their lives.

It was in no sense because of their climate that Tuscany and Umbria set aside the stained-glass window: Romanesque Europe had become aware of the fresco, and the last artist in glass worthy of the masters of Chartres was destined to be Uccello (and the brilliance of his *Resurrection*, when it was revealed at an exhibition in Florence for which the window was taken down, has not—alas!—been conveyed by any reproduction). But this window is unique. The Gothic world was drawing to its close, and the true stained-glass window would not survive the genius of Giotto. It, like mosaics and

132

*97. Peruvian Art - Embroidered Cloak (detail).*

Romanesque tympana, had granted to human forms access to the world of God; now art would be intent on embodying divine forms in the world of men. And the iridescence of stained-glass windows, their relation to a light that lived and was not simply imitated, made it impossible for their genius to survive the new admiration for a painting which was revealing a world of illusion.

It would have seemed that the abstract design of rugs held promise of a brilliant revival for their art. It has not taken place. Are we perhaps on the point of discovering that we term this art decorative because, to us, it has no history, no hierarchy, and no significance? Will color reproduction place it in its proper perspective, classify it, rescue its masterworks from the back rooms of Arab bazaars as Negro sculpture was rescued from the curio shops, liberate Islam from the odium of "backwardness," and assign its due place to this last expression of the undying East? What might we learn if two great exhibitions were to be held, one in Lahore, organized by Moslem specialists, and the other in Paris, organized by Western painters? For that matter, what

98. *Coptic Art - Horseman.*

might we learn from an exhibition of European rugs, also organized by artists? Spanish carpets and French carpets of the Savonnerie are still less well known than those of Persia or the Caucasus. For the time being at least, the carpet seems to be of less interest to our artists than Scythian embroideries or Peruvian or Coptic weavings, though these are actually fabrics of a different nature. When the carpet is considered of interest, it is primarily through its relation to tapestry.

Tapestry itself occupies a place of prime importance in our resurrections. For a long time its decorative nature left it free of any "objective" consideration, and its colors, like those of the stained-glass window, are seldom subordinated to those of what it represents. When its basic material and texture are obliterated by reproduction, it becomes a kind of modern art. We are receptive to a line that is more apparent than that of paintings, to a stiffness reminiscent of wood engravings, to the fluting of its figures, to the scrolls and breaks in the Angers *Apocalypse*, the timid damascening of *La Dame à la Licorne*. (We are rarely indifferent to a rejection of illusion.) In the contrast of their dull reds and night-dark blues, in their whole irrational palette, the oldest tapestries carry on the Romanesque sacred chorale; those of the end of the Middle Ages, and of the Renaissance, provide us with a view of one of the great gentle arts of Christianity.

99. *The Apocalypse - An Angel Shows St. John the Whore of Babylon.*

100. *La Dame à la Licorne - The Sense of Smell.*

But the most spacious realm for the resurrections of the museum without walls is obviously not that of tapestry, or even of the mosaic or the stained-glass window: it is that of the fresco—or, more generally, of mural painting. It forms a part of several civilizations and of several eras of our civilization. Like the statues of the cathedrals, it is sparsely represented in the museum, and often poorly. The frescoes of the Vatican, of the Sistine Chapel, Leonardo's *Last Supper*, have always been renowned, reproduced in copies and in engravings, and are as familiar to artists as any work can become through reproduction. This glory extended no farther back than the earliest of the Sistine works, the flowering of the Quattrocento. The resurrection begins with the "severe style" of Tuscany—Masaccio, Uccello, Castagno, Piero della Francesca—and moves on beyond Giotto, to lose itself, in time, in the Catacombs and in ancient Egypt, and, in space, in Japan.

On the far side of Giotto, it is a resurrection of painting in two dimensions, from Saint-Savin to Palmyra. Almost all of it is religious, or governed by religious forms, in illumination as well as in mural painting: the wall of a church more often than the wall of a palace; a painting born for the church, even when it graces the palace. In it we have not yet done with Byzantium, or with those civilizations for which a hieratic calligraphy could open to the human form the gates of the divine, just as the Latin of the Church opens those same gates to the human word. This transformation of man into a figure in a sacred poem is manifest in countless paintings that we are just beginning to discover: those of the ancient East and of Asia Minor, of the great epochs of Buddhism, those of Etruria, and of Mexico. These paintings, almost all of them frescoes, reveal to us very different palettes. Ochre, blue, and brown of Egypt and Mesopotamia, blue and sanguine of Etruria; the salmon pink of Asia Minor, bedecking the sarcophagi in which Egypt will be buried; the cindery greens and blues, the turquoises, living and dead, of central Asia; the wells of rosy light sunk in areas of darkness, the masses of brown and green of Ajanta; and the lines of these same tones at Nara. These colors are not new to us, but the harmony that exists between them is. We are often charmed by them, and occasionally imprisoned. Within the next twenty years, some frescoes of Egypt and China, of India and the way stations of the Silk Road, along with those that disappeared in the fire at Nara (and the Hokke-ji Buddha, the two great portraits of Takanobu) will have joined a dozen or more Romanesque frescoes in the memory of artists. But are we altogether certain of admiring the cosmic mannerism of the Ajanta frescoes as we admire the sculptures of Ellora, of Elephanta, of

102. *Ajanta (India) - Birth of the Buddha.*

Kanheri? What Romanesque fresco do we consider the equal of the tympana at Moissac or Autun? Christianity's sacred painting was primarily that of the mosaic and the stained-glass window. The continuing expansion of knowledge of the mural painting of churches has done more than just make us familiar with some of the greatest masters of Christendom; it has also modified the perspective in which all of Christian painting once appeared. The same thing does not hold true for earlier painting or for Asiatic painting. And if their resurrection raises fewer, less crucial questions concerning yesterday's museum, even though painting is the major art of our time, it is perhaps because it was not the major art of the civilizations of the sacrosanct.

103. *Ellora (India) - Goddess of the Ganges (detail).* ▶

104. *Berzé-la-Ville -*
*Martyrdom of*
*St. Vincent (detail).*
105. *Moissac - Christ*
*in Majesty (detail).* ▶

106. *Kizil (Central Asia) - A Divinity and a Musician.*
107. *Nara (Japan) - Bodhisattva (detail).*

It is also because, for a long time, the antique exercised an authority in sculpture that it possessed only fleetingly in painting. The antique *is* sculpture: no one would think of comparing the painted decorations of Rome, of Herculaneum, or of Pompeii with the classic statuary so highly venerated by the West. In Baudelaire's time, the antique was the only sculpture admitted into the Louvre.

Let us not forget that, for Baudelaire, sculpture—with the exception of those works of Michelangelo and Puget that were considered contemporary—was a "bastard art," and never entirely ceased being this. He recognized the grandeur of Assyrian and Mexican bas-reliefs without separating it from naïveté; but to him, and to almost all of his friends, medieval sculpture, from the first Romanesque tympanum to the last of the cathedrals, was of so little importance as a form of art that he never spoke of it. The resurrection of this sculpture can in no sense be attributed to Romanticism, which always confused it with the stage settings for *Faust:* it resurrected that portion of it that was a purveyor of dreams, but it never resurrected the true genius of Christendom at its height. The Romantic restorations repaired the façade of the cathedrals while *destroying* the style of their statues. In the Europe of the time, the Middle Age was the fourteenth and primarily the fifteenth centuries: not that of the Christ of Chartres or of the Christ in Majesty of the tympana, but that of horned devils, of a Germany transformed into legend by the engravings of Dürer, which were to symbolize the Middle Age as Goya's were to symbolize Spain. A Gothic art which presumably had known nothing of Romanesque art. Prosper Mérimée, an archaeologist, taught Stendhal the distinction between Romanesque and Gothic art in much the same way as the succession of Chinese styles is taught today. In reading Hugo's *Notre Dame de Paris*, what is there that would make us think of the Royal Portal of Chartres, or even of *The Annunciation* of Amiens, of *The Smile* of Rheims? In the very middle of the nineteenth century, to "save" the tympana of Saint-Denis, sepulcher of the kings of France, the sculptor Brun rounded off the figures of the statuary, obliterating their individual style—and signed his name. Ingres' paintings, including the portrait of Madame Rivière, were termed Gothic. Gautier, passing through Chartres, *did not make a detour* of a quarter of a mile to see the cathedral. On the day of the coronation of Charles X, Victor Hugo made a note of his emotion at the sight of the cathedral of Rheims, but he showed no great concern over the fact that its stone heads had been trimmed "because they were too prominent"; and when he returned to the same cathedral, in 1871, its statuary interested him not at all.

Rodin (in 1910!) deplored the neglect of the Gothic churches. Delacroix, at the age of 57, discovered with surprise that the statues of the cathedral of Strasbourg *"are not really so barbarian,"* and until the day of his death he quoted Poussin's dictum: *"Compared with the ancient Greeks, Raphael is an ass."*

Neither Marx, nor Taine, nor Nietzsche questioned the prestige of the antique: statues that owed nothing to Greece belonged in the field of archaeology.

Since the Europe of the great monarchies never thought of Romano-Hellenistic works as forms of a sacred art, the century that gathered together all of the masterpieces of religious sculpture, including those of Aegina and Olympia, followed on more than three centuries in which the only sculpture of the past worthy of admiration was also the only sculpture considered profane. The fact that the statues of all of the sacred mountains, of all the temples and the tombs, should now have taken the place of the statuary of public squares, of palaces and antique gardens, is enough to suggest that this was more than a matter of a change in esthetic. Since everyone could see the statues of Notre-Dame de Paris, was the discovery of religious sculpture of secondary importance? Everyone may have glanced at those statues, but they did not see them: if they had, Baudelaire and Delacroix would not have ignored them; and Viollet-le-Duc, who was enraptured by the architecture of Notre-Dame, would not have destroyed them. No matter how surprising it may seem to us, the birth of modern art, the destruction of traditional illusionism, symbolized by Manet's *Olympia*, coincides with the destruction of the primacy of the antique, and thus of the exclusive dominion of a profane sculpture.

To Manet and Cézanne, and even to the "three old masters" born with the century—Corot, Ingres, and Delacroix—the most surprising characteristic of our museum without walls would be the irruption of sculpture, the multiple and profound presence with which its past, and not that of painting, has reconstructed the past of all of our art. Obviously, an understanding of the language of Gothic sculpture does not necessarily imply an understanding of that of the Bayon towers of Angkor, of the caves of India, or of the bas-reliefs the Sassanian kings had carved into the flanks of the Iranian mountains; but let us remember that Rodin studied Gothic sculpture, Cambodian dancers, and the bas-reliefs of Angkor with equal care. The kings and saints of the cathedrals were providing us with an introduction to all the sculpture of the world.

Would this epic history, which now fills the museum without walls, have been the same without the transfiguration of sculpture through photography?

These bas-reliefs, these statues, have become plates in an album. The vastly expanded public that welcomes them is unaware of a feeling which, for four centuries, played a large role in the relationship between the collector and the work of art: the feeling of ownership. We do not own the works we admire in reproduction (almost all of them are in museums), and we know that we will never own them, that we will never own anything like them. They are ours because we are artists, just as the statues of medieval saints belonged to the faithful because they were Christian (but these medieval statues were also saints, and our statues are only statues). This indifference to possession that, for us, frees the work of art from its quality of *objet d'art*, also makes us more sensitive than collectors of *objets d'art* to the creative accent of the work, an accent that photography reveals in minor or smaller works as well as in masterpieces. The world of photographs is, unquestionably, only the servant of the world of originals; and yet, appealing less directly to the emotions and far more to the intellect, it seems to reveal or to "develop"— in the sense in which this word is used in photography—the creative act; to make of the history of art primarily a continuing succession of creations.

But this intellectualized world possesses its own sources of emotion because none of these plates exhausts the work it represents. In order to interpret it, they must compensate for a depth they do not themselves possess; [1] and in doing so they give it a more intense form of life than could be achieved in a cast reproduction. This is especially true in the case of statues that have remained in their original locations, where photography can suggest the grotto, the cathedral, the mountain. In substituting the album for the gallery of a museum, it awakens the vaguely troubled lyricism induced by a meeting between works separated by half the surface of the globe but brought to us still wearing remnants of their forests, their desert, their mountains—and induced also by the contribution made by the angle, the distance, and the time of day chosen by the photographer. Dawn and dusk make of the Sphinx an actor playing the role of the Sphinx.

[1] It is the impossibility of solving a problem of this nature that has—thus far— prevented the museum without walls from including architecture within its realm. The exterior of monuments becomes too small: reproduction imposes on them a scale that would be equally unsuited to statues or to large paintings if it were imposed on them. As for the interior of cathedrals, temples, and even palaces, photography, although it has long been capable of conveying relief, has not yet (with the exception of some few successes) arrived at the point of conveying depth—although the cinema occasionally suggests it.

148

114. *Teotihuacan (Mexico) - Head of a Plumed Serpent.*

Like the reading of a play, as distinct from seeing it performed, or listening to a phonograph record, as distinct from hearing the same piece in a concert hall (but also like the reading of plays we will never see performed, listening to records of concerts we will never hear), there is now appearing, outside the walls of the museum and distinct from its contents, the broadest artistic domain man has known, the first heritage of all of history—including history as yet unknown.

A heritage that has been extended even further, in the past few years, by retrospective exhibitions, those brilliant and fleeting dependencies of the museum without walls. (In Paris alone, in the period from 1958 to 1964, there were such exhibitions of the work of Poussin and Delacroix, of Coptic art, and of the art of Iran, India, Mexico, and Japan.) And, within their limits, even the museums of collections of casts and copies are expanding the boundaries of this heritage: in 1937— when Braque and Picasso were both almost 60— the fresco section of the French national monuments first revealed the color of the Romanesque frescoes. These museums also bring together widely dispersed works. They make their selections broadly because they are not obliged to acquire the originals they copy. They are arbiters of the confrontations that occur within their walls. They have more impact than the album, but do not possess to the same degree the virus that separates individual works to the benefit of style, since this stems from their common reduction to the format of the book, from the proximity and the succession of the plates, which animates a style as time-lapse photography animates the growth of a plant. These museums, and the large scale exhibitions as well, are now in the process of finding their own photographic expression.

And the cities of art have become the new cities of pilgrimage.

Like the reproductions in the album that will record their brief passage, the works on display in the exhibition have lost their function—from the golden plates on which no king any longer dines to the gods to whom no priest any longer prays. And the function of the museum, is that lost too? A museum rarely possesses the historic continuity of an exhibition to which twenty nations have contributed, or of an album, or of the totality of the museum without walls; no museum reveals to us to such an extent a long sequence of works attaining a vitality that stems *from their sequence*, as though some genie of art had urged on the same tide of conquest from illumination to stained-glass window, from stained glass to fresco, from fresco to picture. When seen through the ambiguous unity of photography, the Mesopotamian style, from the *Fertilities* of the tombs to the cylinder seals, to the bas-reliefs, to the statues and bronze plaques of the nomads, seems to take on a creative existence of its own. This same ambiguous unity brings about the appearance of those imagined super-artists we term styles, and to whom we grant an obscure birth, a life, some victories, some defeats, a term of agony, and occasionally a renaissance or a resurrection.

The pluralism with which Moissac, Ellora, and Sumer seemed to face the autocracy of Athens is not simply an extension of that which opposed Rubens to Raphael. The reproductions in monograph albums bring into focus the intent and significance of a painter as secret as Vermeer, as complex as Rembrandt, as well as those of a painter as extroverted as Rubens. But Rubens (and, more significantly, Rembrandt) was and still is placed in comparison with Raphael, simply as an individual: although they do not belong to the same national culture or to the same century, they belong to the same civilization, and artists, who are seldom affected by determinist doctrine, compared them as they once compared Delacroix with Ingres and still compare Braque with Picasso. But it is neither a difference in individual expression nor a rivalry—even a rivalry on the level of genius—that opposes the head of the Pharaoh Zoser or the statues of Gudea to the Buddhas of Lung-Men, the figures of Elephanta to the *Charioteer* of Delphi, and Dogon or Congolese masks to the faces on the Royal Portal. The artist of the great religious styles who was almost always anonymous, seems more possessed by his gods than master of his work; above all, the capital significance of his art scarcely belongs to him, because it belongs primarily to his faith—especially when that faith is not our own. Poussin's vision could be, and was, compared with that of Rubens, but it could not be compared with that of the Byzantine mosaicists or of African sculptors: their art is not the expression of a vision, but of the invisible.

It seems evident to us that a style can be the legitimate, resurrected expression of the creative intent, whose meaning unites the artists of a civilization like an all-embracing spirit; but we are forgetting that Europe and the rest of the world discovered this fact in the twentieth century. To the Crusaders, the Sphinx at Gizeh was simply a devil, as the Aztec gods were devils to the Spaniards. For three centuries, Greece, Rome, Florence, and Venice represented to Europe the master schools of a style which rejected all others. The classicism of the great monarchies had known only the past of its own art; it had preserved its Byzantine art and its medieval art—when it did preserve them—through reverence, as it preserved its Romanesque black Virgins. The classicisms of Asia scorned all European art: to each his own form of the grotesque. The Louvre of the Romanticist age seemed somewhat more receptive, but it followed the example of the collections that had preceded it and accepted only its own precursors; while the greatest artists of the time still spoke of Egyptian naïveté. The Louvre itself had accepted Egypt and Chaldea, but only in their quality as dependencies of the Bible and of antiquity. The perception of a high intent, of an essential significance, has freed all of the civilizations foreign to our own from the prejudice of clumsiness, 161 just as it led to the "discovery" of El Greco and of Grünewald. Precursors are not absent from the vast, and constantly varying, treasury of the museum without walls; but we think of every great style as the symbol of a fundamental relationship between man and the universe, of a civilization with the value it holds supreme: with its gods. The past of art, which to Europe had been only the past of *one* style termed art, appears to us as a world of styles; in it, artistic creation becomes the means by which forms become style. A power that was ignored or disdained a century ago is revealed as one of the major powers of the artist; and its expression as one of the major characteristics of art. But the dazzling ascent of that power has brought with it an obscure realization of something we are not likely to forget again: the museum was an affirmation, the museum without walls is an interrogation.

A resurrection of this kind inevitably gathers together works that have undergone a profound metamorphosis. And primarily, in the real museum, as well as on the heights of the Acropolis, in the caves of India, or on the portals of cathedrals, works in which time has wrought many changes.

Almost all of the past has reached us without its colors. The majority of the statues of the Eastern Empire were painted, as were those of Central Asia, of India, of China, and of Japan; the art of Rome was often of all the variegated colors of marble. Romanesque statues, Gothic statues—painted. Pre-Columbian idols, it seems, were painted; and so were Mayan bas-reliefs.

The vestiges of Greek colors suggest a world very different from that which Hellenic sculpture has so long suggested. The word Greece comes to us through Alexandria, but those elements of Alexandrian art we have allowed to stand as Greek are difficult to reconcile with figures painted in three colors. The palette of an epoch is no less a part of that epoch than its drawing; but even though each of us can comprehend an evolution of line that passes from Gothic rigidity to the arabesque of the Renaissance and the frenzy of the Baroque, the recognized link between a civilization and its color amounts to little more than an idea—cautiously vague—that the painting of so-called harmonious civilizations will be clear and light, and that of dualistic civilizations, dark. The Mayan frescoes are clear, however, and so are many of the recast skulls of Oceania and the Manichaean miniatures. The idea, therefore, would seem to be on a par with believing that the music of heroic ages is made up of military marches. The color of a sculpture that is itself indifferent to realism is rarely realistic: Greek statues were polychrome, but Plato tells us that in his time the pupils of their eyes were painted *red*. The provinces of color in the great civilizations of the past were as specific and as unpredictable as their provinces of forms, but with the relative exception of Egypt they are no longer indicated to us by anything more than fragments, and our vast resurrection has often altered the language of these survivors. A coherent system has taken the place of the original system, but it is no less likely to survive.

We know, therefore—we sense—that Greek statues and a great many Mesopotamian statues have come to us transformed. But what of Roman-

esque art—whose resurrection follows on that of the ancient world and surpasses it? Its columns were ribboned with vivid colors; certain of its Christs were as dazzling as Polynesian fetishes, and its most renowned tympana were painted in accord with the palette of the manuscript illuminations of their day. Their colors, no more realist than those of the stained-glass window, of the archaic Greeks, or of the clay Buddhas, expressed a world that is beginning to be revealed to us in Romanesque frescoes; a very different world from that of monochrome churches. Gothic ended with the medley of color in the base of a Calvary—Sluter's *Well of Moses:* Moses' robe was red, the lining of his mantle, blue; the pedestal was spangled with initials and with golden suns, and painted, as was the entire Calvary, by Malouel. The figure of Job wore real spectacles of gold. (This doubtful illusion was to reappear in the polychrome woodcarvings of Spain.) The museums of all of Central Europe make it clear to us that there existed, in the Middle Ages, a form of cinema in colors; and there is present evidence of it in the multicolored fountains in the towns and hamlets of Germany.

When the painting that covered Romanesque wooden statues is apparent to us at all, it is transformed at the very least by a patina of time, and always by decay; and the transformation brought about by both the one and the other affects the very nature of the sculpture. Our taste is as sensitive to the subtle decomposition of colors intended to dazzle the eye as that of the last century was to the thick varnishes of the museums. If a well-preserved Romanesque Virgin and a time-scarred Virgin of Auvergne seem to us to belong to the same art, it is not because the Auvergne Virgin is a mutilated replica of the other, but because the intact Virgin shares, in a lesser degree, the quality we recognize in the ravaged Virgin. This is all the more true because medieval statues are not intact: either they derive from their decomposition a quality similiar to that which bronzes owe to their patina, or they have been repainted in the course of the centuries (and not only those of Europe). It is this that is responsible for the falsely naïve appearance of so many Romanesque and Gothic figures of Spain and Italy. This appearance vanishes with restoration, which is carefully planned not to scrape or scour the work entirely, but simply to uncover whatever remains of the original polychrome, and thereby restore the "presence of time." We are as sensitive to the mutilation of color as our forebears were to the mutilation of statuary. But this feeling for the exquisite smaller object does not prevail against the Royal Portal of Chartres: as recently as 1950 no album of any great importance was devoted to Romanesque polychrome sculpture. For our Romanesque art is an art       165

119-120. *Bologna - Crucifixion (Before and After Restoration)*.

of stone, an art of the bas-relief and the statue-column: an art of monuments. In our admiring eyes, it has become monochrome, *as was the art of the ancient world* in the eyes of Michelangelo... Since an intact grouping of *The Descent from the Cross* often substitutes the accent of a Christmas *crèche* or a Breton wayside Calvary for the true majesty of Romanesque, we are in no more haste to restore the Calvary of Erill-la-Vall than the arms of the *Victory of Samothrace*. The mutilation that forms a part of the glorious perfection of the *Venus de Milo* might be the work of an antiquarian who was also a genius; even mutilations have their style. A process of filtration, which it would be too simple to call taste, contributes to our resurrection: ever since the Quattrocento, collections of antiques have acquired torsos more happily than legs. We often prefer the statues of Lagash if the head is gone, Khmer Buddhas without legs, and Assyrian beasts only in isolation. Chance may shatter and time bring metamorphosis, but it is we who choose.

167

◀ 118. *Saint-Denis - Virgin and Child*.

*121. Erill-la-Vall (Catalonia) - Descent from the Cross.*

The evolution of museums, and the birth of the museum without walls, would be more comprehensible if we understood clearly that they are linked with a metamorphosis of the work of art that is not founded entirely on the development of our own knowledge: the West had been familiar with fetishes and idols for a long time when it first discovered Negro and Mexican art. The quality of metamorphosis in the work of art succeeds what was termed its quality of immortality, just as our resurrection of millennia succeeds the Renaissance of a few centuries of the past.

*122. Mitgaran (Catalonia) - Torso of Christ.* ▶

And yet the art which revealed the existence of this immortality and was claimed as antecedent by this Renaissance—Greek art—still occupies the place of honor in our museums; as though the broadening realm of our knowledge had served only to increase our admiration. For four centuries Europe revered Greek art above all others, and we admire it still; but we do not admire the same statues, we are not referring to the same Greece.

For us the fundamental revelation of Greece is her constant questioning of the nature of the universe. These philosophers who taught the art of living, these gods who changed with their statues—as submissive to artists as dreams —had altered the very meaning of art. Despite the evolution of forms that, from century to century, had asserted ever more clearly in Egypt the invincible order of the stars and the eternal, and in Assyria of blood, art had been only the visible symbol of a response, made to destiny once and for all by each civilization. And then, in the space of fifty years, the stubborn question that was the very voice of Greece destroyed this Tibetan litany. Greek art is the first art which seems to us profane, since it marks the end of singularity and the triumph of the multiplicity of the world, the end of the supreme value of contemplation and of the psychic states in which man thinks to attain the absolute by surrendering himself to the rhythms of the cosmos and losing himself in their oneness. The fundamental passions now take on their human zest; exaltation assumes the name of joy. The sacred dance in which the forms of Hellas make their first appearance is the dance of mankind at last shaking off the yoke of destiny.

In this, Greek tragedy misleads us. The fatality of the House of Atreus is actually the end of the great oriental fatalities. Here, the gods show as much concern for men as men for the gods. These figures from the depths are not rooted in the eternity of the Babylonian sand; they free themselves from it when men do, as men do. In the destiny of man, man comes into his own and destiny ends. To a devout Moslem, even today, the tragedy of Oedipus is much ado about nothing: how look on Oedipus as an ill-starred exception, when every man is Oedipus? And in the art that made tragic drama of the tragic themes so known to the Athenian people, it was not the defeat of man they admired, but, on the contrary, his eventual triumph in the poet's subjugation of destiny.

Within every artichoke is an acanthus leaf, and the acanthus is what man would have made of the artichoke, had God asked his advice. Greece chose her own forms, and then brought them, step by step, to the measure of man, just as she brought back to this measure the forms of foreign arts: there can

171

125. *Greek Art - Head of Athena.*

◀ 124. *Egyptian Art - The Pharaoh Zoser (detail).*

be little doubt that a landscape by Apelles would suggest a landscape made by man and not by the cosmos. The elements of the cosmos are humanized, the oriental stars forgotten: by contrast with the towering immobility of Asiatic statuary, the unprecedented movement of Greek statues is the symbol of man's new freedom. The Greek nude was to be a nude, a nude released from bondage, one that might have been created by a god who had not ceased to be a man.

It is this conquest of the bondage of the past that makes us pause in front of the *Koré of Euthydikos* and the *Head of a Youth* in the Acropolis Museum, just as it makes us pause before the *Athena* of Aegina. Their style is known as the severe style; but even before their birth, on statues whose origins are uncertain but whose style retained an archaic frontalism, artists had sketched something unknown to Egypt or to Mesopotamia, to Iran, or to any art before: the smile.

Far more than in the rippling line of its draperies, Greece is personified in this gentle curve of the lips, which calls up visions of the Odyssey, and which is not the "internal smile"— that smile which seems to have no connection with laughter—of Buddhism and of some Egyptian heads; for, whether it be primitive or complex, the smile of Greece is meant for the person who sees it and turns back to look. Whenever it recurs, something of Greece is on the point of bursting into flower, whether in the smile of Rheims or in that of Florence; and whenever he becomes master of his destiny, man reconquers the fleeting majesty he conquered for the first time on the mountain at Delphi.

If, to us, the female nude of Greece suggests sensual pleasure, it is because we realize at once that it has been freed of ritual paralysis, and all of its movements are simply suspended, as the movements of the living are suspended in sleep; but above all it is because the order of the stars to which it is linked has ceased to be fatality and become harmony, because an Earth which has now become a mother has reached out to the cosmos itself in its triumph over the awesome domination of the Goddess-Mothers. And when we cease to regard it with Christian eyes, when we compare it, not to the Gothic nude but to the Indian nude, its accent promptly changes: its eroticism fades into the background; we discover that it radiates freedom, that its splendid forms are invisibly clothed in the draperies of Victories.

The artist of the East—and the Byzantine artist, centuries later—had translated the visible world into a style that subordinated it to the world of the invisible, a style governed by values whose most constant element was that

126. *Victory of Samothrace.* ▶

127. *Khajuraho (India)*
   *- Nayika (detail)*.

128. *The Venus of Cnidos*
*(Ancient Replica of Praxiteles).*

of the eternal. Hellenic art finds its strength in its harmony with man, as the arts of destiny and the eternal found theirs in their discord: they sought neither art nor beauty; they did not have "a style"; they were style. Greek

129. *Attributed to Pythagoras of Rhegium - The Charioteer (detail)*. 130. *Praxiteles - Hermes (detail)*.

art, in its conflict with the art of the ancient East, and the Christian arts, in their conflict with the oriental influence on Christianity, followed similar paths to the discovery of representation. The flowing line that takes the place of the sharp angles of the severe style—notably in the lips and the lids of the eyes—foreshadows Leonardo's suppression of outline. The pagan gods were to will to Italy the technique of an idealizing illusionism. And it is this legacy that forms the background to the passionate dialogue between Italian art and antiquity that began when Italy, in her turn, substituted admiration for reverence and began to seek in art the exemplary image of woman and the convincing depiction of heroes. Antiquity, and nothing more: neither Etruscan art nor the successive styles of Greece, but the ensemble of Hellenistic works and Roman copies, which expressed a symbolic and global antiquity. Lysippus, in depicting Alexander, also expressed Themistocles. Until the first exhibition of the fragments brought to London by

Lord Elgin, the glory of Phidias was based on contemporary texts: Michelangelo, who was overwhelmed when he saw the *Laocoön*, never saw any of the figures from the Parthenon; and neither did Poussin. For them, the history of Greek art was the history of an exemplary idealization, unequalled by any other. The barbarian world had been ignorant of it; the civilized world had resurrected it. The supreme style was also the immortal style, of which others were no more than the infancy or the decline. The great sculpture, the only true sculpture, was that of antiquity. Michelangelo and Donatello thought thus, and so did Canova, whose reaction to the fragments of the Parthenon was one of stunned astonishment. To our own astonishment, even Delacroix thought thus.

This antique sculpture is that of the *deserted* galleries of our museums. But even when it dazzled Michelangelo, it was the product of a fundamental metamorphosis. Often as a result of mutilation, or the presence of a patina on the bronzes, which Greece had always removed—in other words, the presence of time; for the first time in a thousand years, this was the presence of immortality, and no longer that of death. And also because of the absence of the décor that had surrounded these figures of gods and goddesses and of emperors who had decreed themselves divine; above all, because they were all reborn to a world that no longer recognized their divinity. Even if Alexandria had been somewhat absent-minded in its belief in Venus, Venus had been a part of its civilization; her image had existed in men's souls, it was not born of an artist's invention. It was a part of an age-old dream, not simply a nude who might have been the artist's mistress. If the *Aphrodite* of Praxiteles was a deified portrait of Phryne, it was because Phryne had here become Aphrodite. Art in Greece had been the means of giving form to the gods, and in Italy these gods became the figures that gave form to the privileged realm of art.

The antiquity that was reborn as an idealization of vanished or imagined models was now related only to the world of the living—and to art. The museum without walls was born of a metamorphosis as profound as that which gave birth to the first Italian collections; and like the gods of antiquity at the time of the Renaissance, the gods who are being resurrected for us today are shorn of their divinity.

If their original spirits might in some way be restored to these statues, the museums would call forth a prayer more vast than any the world has known; if we experienced the emotions felt by the first men to view the God-King of Egypt in his statuary double, or by the first men to raise their eyes to a

Romanesque crucifix, we could not leave either crucifix or statues to the Louvre. We know that all the arts of the sacred, all the arts of faith, have been swept up in the tide of metamorphosis; that to the Christian Cézanne a Romanesque crucifix was a piece of sculpture and not Christ, Cimabue's *Madonna* a painting and not the Virgin Mary; that the statues of the Pharaohs no longer represent the double of a god to anyone. From the gods of Sumer to our angels and our saints, all of these arts have expressed a world whose existence was more real than that of the earth, because it was that of the eternal. Their creation has resulted in the emptying of the galleries of antiques —but not of those in which Florence and Rome expressed a genius they believed to be rooted in a dialogue with antiquity. To us, Italy's resurrection of Myth, and primarily of Venus, seems to have been taken as a license to paint those things that exist for no one, to give them, through art, a value equal to that of the figures of faith; and then to paint men and saints, the Virgin and Christ, even landscapes, as if they were reflections of a wondrous world of the unreal. At this moment of time in Italy, the metamorphosis seems to have come to a halt, making way for a more simple process of inheritance. But even though Athens may swarm with unprecedented numbers of tourists, our chosen Greece ends at the Parthenon—where, yesterday, Europe's Greece began.

The expression of the world of the unreal forms a close and deliberate bond between poetic creation and artistic creation. Most modern works on art, oriented by the specific character of our contemporary arts, have disregarded the union of these two creations.[1] We might as well disregard Christ in attempting to understand the sculpture of cathedrals. The domain of poetry that originates in works of art is obscure, because it mingles Sumer and the Acropolis, Venice and Memphis, Ajanta, Chartres, Florence, the caves of India on the banks of their slow-moving rivers, and Mexican ruins amid the tangled vegetation of a tropic land; Michelangelo, Piero della Francesca and the master of the Avignon *Pietà*, Rembrandt and the sculptor of Cheops ... simple enumeration of the cities of art resembles a poem from *Légende des Siècles*. The great religious works are inseparable from a powerful poetry, and become poetry to the extent that they become art when they are no longer documents of truth, but their poetry is always subordinated to faith and, almost always, is a means of expression of faith. But in the art

[1] Between 1950 and 1960 statements by artists ranging from Braque to Soulages— three generations—have accorded a high place to poetry.

131. *Piero de Cosimo - The Death of Procris.*

of the unreal (as in certain of the arts of the Far East), painting becomes a means of expression of poetry—and often its preferred means of expression. Shakespeare was born the year of Michelangelo's death, but what poets of the Renaissance can be compared with Botticelli, Piero di Cosimo, Leonardo, or the great Venetians? And what French poetry of the time of Watteau is the peer of his painting?

The distinction that is made today between the specific characteristics of painting and its characteristics as poetry is as indefinite as the distinction between form and content. They once comprised an indivisible domain.

"Painting,"Leonardo wrote, "is poetry that *can be seen.*" From the earliest of the Tuscan mythologies to the last days of Venice, Italian painting is one of the most manifest poetic enterprises the world has known. In Persia and the Indies, painting that does not illustrate sacred texts illustrates poems; in the Far East, the poem forms a part of the landscape, and it would be impossible to grasp the full meaning of the work without it. Rather than exclude poetry from painting, we should recognize that all great works of plastic art are steeped in poetry. When a realist is also possessed of genius, poetry comes to him even though he has not sought it. How can we fail to see the poetry of Vermeer, of Chardin, of Breughel, and of the great Courbets? Is it only their color that we admire in Titian and Hieronymus Bosch? Realistic as Bosch's color may seem, it links his *Juggler* with the reflection of the fires he has built on the snowy plains of hell; and a magical fantasy is no more separable from Titian's painting than an infernal fantasy is separable from that of the Flemish "maker of devils." Are Rembrandt's portraits and almost

181

132. *Niccoló dell'Abbate - The Abduction of Persephone (detail).*

all of Hals's separated only by the difference in two palettes? And is that all that separates the *Governors of the Almshouse* in Haarlem from *The Shooting Company?* The fantasy reaches its climax in the most unreal city of Europe, in the dreamlike ballet of Guardi.

It is, in fact, through a dreamlike quality more profound than Guardi's that our own time (after a period of reaction against the Romanticists and pre-Raphaelite exaggeration) is now groping toward a rediscovery of the poetry of painting: a quality that links the world of dreams with a truly pictorial expression, such as that of Bosch or Piero di Cosimo, or, in a different realm, such as that of the deliberately poetic adventure that was often the foundation of mannerism. The elongation of figures, the transparency of veils, an arabesque so often related more closely to gem carvings than to Alexandria, and an arbitrary use of color are all essentially plastic means of expression, even when Myth is queen. It was the mannerists who invented the dissonant

133. *Bosch - The Temptation of St. Anthony (detail).* ▶

harmony that was later to be taken up again by the Spanish painters of the Baroque. But all these incarnations of Venus and Diana, resembling a Danaë as haughtily detached as a cameo, form a part of the poetic mystery of *Eva Prima Pandora*, of Gourmont's *La Cave*, of Caron's *La Sémelé*, of the dark

134. *Rembrandt - The Painter and His Model.*

horses of the chariot that carries Niccoló dell'Abbate's *Persephone* into the underworld kingdom of Pluto.

We are automatically receptive to this kind of poetry because it is in fundamental agreement with the poetry of our time. We know that Piero di Cosimo is a brother to Chirico; we have discovered the unfinished etchings in which Rembrandt expresses our own sense of mystery. But let us make no mistake about his.

Our sectarian poetry willingly fashioned its universe to accord with perspectives of the dream and the irrational. No doubt all poetry is irrational in the sense that it substitutes a new system of relationships for the "established" relation of things to each other. But this victory, long before it usurped the solitude of an artist, had been only a minor element of a vast upheaval, the fevered victory of the joys of earth or of the star-strewn night

135. *Michelangelo - Night (detail)* ▶

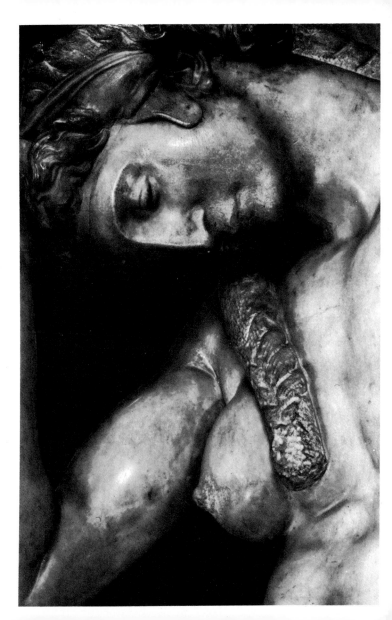

136. *Leonardo da Vinci - Saint-Anne, the Virgin and the Child (detail).*

137. *Rembrandt - The Return of the Prodigal Son (detail)*.

over the brooding presence of the Goddess-Mothers or the sleep of the gods. Mallarmé is not a greater poet than Homer or Shakespeare; or Piero di Cosimo than Titian. The dream has not always vanquished the poem of exaltation: Baudelaire's *Night* joins forces with Michelangelo's, it does not efface it.

After having been a means to the creation of a sacrosanct universe, painting, for several centuries, was chiefly a means to the conquest of a universe that was not exclusively pictorial. Subjects were referred to as "big"—and the adjective conveys a whole attitude. When modern art was born, official painting had replaced this conquest with the subordination of the artist to a romantic or sentimental spectacle, often rooted in history—to a form of theater freed from its cramped stage, if not from its gestures. Reacting against this realism of the imaginary, painting found its way back to poetry by ceasing to illustrate the poectic whims of historians and refusing to cater to those of an indifferent public: *by creating its own*. Cézanne's *Montagne Noire*, Renoir's *Moulin de la Galette*, Gauguin's *Cavaliers sur la Plage*, Chagall's

188

138. *Meissonier - "1814".*

139. *Rouault - The Old King.* ▶

*Fables*, Dufy's sunlit holidays, Klee's sharp-angled phantoms do not derive their poetry from what they represent, but make use of what they represent to focus their specific poetry. It is Goya's drawing that speaks to us, not the depiction of the innumerable martyrs of Baroque academicism. And Piero, and Rembrandt ... we allow ourselves to be seduced by the harmony of pinks and grays in *L'Enseigne de Gersaint*, but not by the appeal of Boucher or of some Alexandrine to our sensuality, of Greuze or some Bolognese painter to our sentimentality: by Rouault's *Le Vieux Roi*, but not by Meissonier's Napoleon on the muddy road of *"1814"*. If the subjects of the Salon artists are fictitious, it is because, far from being given life by the art of those who painted them, they are models to which this art submits itself. Titian did not "reproduce" imagined scenes, he wrested Venus from the night of Cadore. Leonardo, Rembrandt, Goya seek and find both poetic and pictorial expression, often simultaneously. Pisanello's hanged men, the sunlit distances of Leonardo, and the nocturnal depths of Bosch, Rembrandt's light, and Goya's phantoms are both poetry and painting. *The Prodigal Son* is given life by Rembrandt's art, Cytherea by Watteau's, a host of apparitions by Goya's, and *Night* by Michelangelo's. Poetry comes as naturally to this art as the flower to a plant.

The expression of this poetry, however, has undergone a metamorphosis akin to that experienced by the expressions of the sacred of Sumer and of Egypt, by the faith of the Romanesque, and especially by the Hellenic concept of the divine. Even though the object—picture or statue—is little altered in itself; even though it belongs to a civilization of which ours is a direct descendant, the nature of the work has changed. Similar in that respect to the bas-relief of the Panathenaea, where the first butterfly came to rest, Botticelli's *Venus*, Donatello's *David*, Michelangelo's *Night*, Verrocchio's *Colleoni* will never again be unlooked-for apparitions. Like the power of revelation induced by the first stunning images of the Sumerian gods and the first countenance in which Christ became something more than a symbol, the demiurgic power of the masters of the unreal is, to us, no longer anything but an artistic power. In their metamorphosis, the inhabitants of the world of the unreal mingle with the peoples of faith, and *Night*, like the crucifix, has become sculpture; Danaë, like the Virgin, has become a painting.

Like the Virgin—and like the portrait, the landscape, and the still life: the same form of metamorphosis affects, in varying degrees, those things which have their roots in the earth and those which derive from the dream or the heavens.

Europe calls two different arts "realist." One is characterized by values opposed to spiritualization or idealization: some Gothic figures, Caravaggio, Goya, the Bamboccianti. The other, by an illusionism whose master, independently of his genius, is Jan Van Eyck: the realism of the miserable and the illusionism of *trompe l'œil*.

Obviously, the major part of the interest aroused by illusionism stems from the portrait, not from *trompe l'œil*. Whether or not it seems free of its own time, the portrait frees its model from time; the first great Western portraits, in liberating the human face from time and death, were doubtless no less unexpected apparitions than the incarnations of Venus. Islam's violent reaction to representation of the human form is based, at least in part, on the fact that painted figures do not grow old—on the artist's victory over death. No matter how great the power of imitation of its author may be, the portrait does not escape its own time: we say that Van Eyck has never been surpassed in this respect, but we describe his portraits as primitives. In the case of *Giovanni Arnolfini and his Bride* this would seem to be self-evident, because of the setting, the costumes, the furnishings; it is much less self-evident in *The Man with the Red Turban*. Even if Van Eyck thought that he was referring to nothing but his model, he was also referring to the Flemish religious painting that preceded his, and his portraits are portraits of donors who have lost their saints. In addition to this, we consider the composition, the relationship of the figure to its background, as a part of the history of art. The means of illusion through which later portraits—those of Rubens, for example—relegated Van Eyck's to the past are not means of imitation, but of suggestion: foreshortening, lighting, space, and even a certain freedom in the brushwork; in short, the suggestion of possible movement, the feeling of an immobility *seized* and not *posed* (a feeling that is so powerfully expressed in the drawing of the Far East, where *trompe l'œil* is unknown). A Rubens portrait is not intended to arouse the same emotions as a portrait by Van Eyck, even in its model. And all efforts toward realist art are inseparable from an intention of which imitation is only the means. This intention, which animates all the realism of misery and monsters, is often inspired by the struggle against an idealization, but it no more escapes either time or metamorphosis than the idealization it is battling. We can date realist works as easily as works of idealization, and neither the still lifes nor even the *trompes l'œil* of the eighteenth century can be confused with those of the fifteenth. The same tide of metamorphosis sweeps over Caravaggio's bowl of fruit, his stable boy saints, and the Virgins of the Carracci.

But Caravaggio's bowl of fruit is an easel painting, and so are the majority of realist scenes. These works are portable, generally destined for the rooms of ordinary houses; if their metamorphosis seems less obvious to us than

140. *Egyptian Art - Renefer (detail).*

that of different forms of work, it is because, among other reasons, a canvas moves easily from a seventeenth-century Dutch house to the Amsterdam Museum, while a statue moves less easily from an Egyptian tomb to the Cairo Museum.

The private possession of statues and pictures, their status as a part of the furnishings that surround them, has made us forget or ignore the fact that most civilizations created the work of art for a sanctified place. For several centuries this was the palace. But in a more profound, often more

141. *Egyptian Art - Osiris.*

lasting—and more revealing—sense, it has been the underground vault, the sanctuary, the façade of the temple, the tomb, and the sacred grotto. For these are not places simply of luxury and prestige, but of another world. This is apparent to us at first sight of a cathedral, and in all of the tombs of Egypt that remain where they were built.

In the underground burial chamber, the sculptor has obviously carved a statue destined to open the way for the deceased it represents, to a world different from that of the earth, to a world of eternity: to another world. The function of the statue as an object is to represent the deceased; the function of Egyptian artistic creation, and that of the whole of Egyptian style, is the creation of forms through which the deceased does *not* become a corpse (the rigidity of Egyptian forms is common to all of the sacred arts), but a figure betrothed to eternity. This statue is in no sense an imitation (as a photograph might be said to be) somehow endowed, through accident or genius, with a particular aura: it was carved *to be a double;* its creator might judge it superior, as a double, to some other statue, but if it ceases to be a double it is no longer anything. It belongs to a specific world, of eternity and not of the earth: the world of burial chambers and funerary statues. The sculptor, when he set to work, undertook an image of Prince Re-hotep, of General Renefer, of Queen Nefretete; he also undertook a statue destined to compete with statues of a precisely determined significance, in a predetermined place.

The same thing holds true of all the arts we have resurrected; and, more subtly, of those we have inherited. It is not a question of the harmony of sculpture or painting with a form of architecture (the caves of Asia have no architecture), but with a supernatural place, with the presence of gods, of demons, of the dead. This harmony between the Mesopotamian or Mexican high relief and the sanctuary is obvious, as it is between the Assyrian or Persian bas-relief and the sacred palace, between Hindu, Buddhist, or Sassanian sculpture and the mountain, between the Byzantine mosaic and the Christian basilica. It is less obvious between Gothic sculpture and the cathedral. But even though the Virgin of Rheims may resemble a farm girl of Champagne (but don't the "doubles" of Renefer and Tut-ankh-amen resemble their models?) she is not a farm girl conceived for a palace, for a museum, or for "art." All of the major forms of Gothic art were developed and elaborated for the cathedral, which was to the world of its time what the mosque was until only yesterday: at the center of a tangle of little streets, the vast and solemn world of God. An other-worldly place, as was the Romanesque or Byzantine sanctuary, and the man-made temple, which suceeded those in the caverns of India; and as, to other ends, the Sumerian tomb or the burial chamber once had been. We would have been intrigued by this aspect of the cathedral sooner than we were, if it were not for the ambiguity created by the frame, which was born with Western painting of modern times, and, more precisely, with easel painting. No one would dare set a Hindu, Buddhist, or Romanesque fresco in a traditional frame. These frescoes were not isolated, as they appear on the wall of a museum: in Ajanta, at Saint-Savin, in the Scrovegni chapel, they were incorporated into the sanctuary (despite the occasional presence of bordering elements), just as mosaics and stained-glass windows had been. The independence of the scene seems to originate with the mobility of the picture.

The frame is unkown to the Eastern Christian church: the jeweled casing of an ikon is not a frame; as a part of the ikonostasis, it forms a link with the sanctuary; it is the opposite of the imaginary "open window," which might define a Western painting. But this painting did not have its origins in an open window, even an imaginary one; it was born, like the ikon, with its

142. *Nicolás Francés - Retable of the Virgin (detail).*

143. *Van der Weyden - Retable of the Seven Sacraments (central panel)*.

encasing shell: it was born as a retable. And the frame of the retable was never intended as an embellishment of its separate elements: its role was to maintain or assure the link between the spectacle presented by the religious painting and the place of the religion itself. If so many retables resemble fragments of cathedrals, it is not as a result of any quest for unity of style, such as those that would take place later; it is because these gables, these pinnacles, contrib-

ute to a maintenance in the world of God of a religious image that seemed to be slipping ever further into the world of men. They surround the painting, but they are also often in the painting. In the fifteenth century, the nave of the cathedral became the *background* against which the Madonna, and even the Crucifixion, was pictured. When "nature" (the illusionist nature discovered by Italy and Flanders, not the rocky Byzantine landscape inherited from the mosaics, which is to the later forms of nature what the Virgin of the ikons is to the Virgin of the sixteenth century) replaced the imaginary cathedral as a background for the sacred scenes of the paintings, the frame appeared, but sacred painting vanished. It had been created as a part of a union, in body as in soul, with the sacred place to which it belonged.

The façade of the Parthenon—which crowned the Panathenaean ceremonies as the altar of the cathedral sanctified its processionals—and its classic setting had provided their art with the background and spirit the sacred places had provided for the sacred arts. Phidias had sculpted his *Athena* for the Acropolis. Roman palaces had undoubtedly endowed the statues created for them with the appearance of an oppressive, unreal world, whose ghost would later be invoked by Piranesi. The Vatican, the palace of the doges, the palace of Versailles make it clear to us that the influence exerted on art by the cathedrals of the unreal is not limited to architecture or to the decorative arts. If we are not clearly aware of the extent of the metamorphosis imposed on images created for the tomb, the sanctuary, or the cathedral by their transfer into the museum or the museum without walls, it is because Europe, forgetting the supernatural place for which they were created, welcomed them in the same way in which it welcomed all of the works it had thus far chosen. In the Louvre, they were in another sanctified place— the museum itself; but, considered as interpretations of the models they represented, they were now in the company of the *Venus de Milo* and the paintings of the Salon Carré, and shared in their glory. When an Egyptian or medieval statue entered the Louvre as a companion to the statues already gathered there, it was thought of as having been related to a "model"; all were considered as being related to what Giotto called nature.

Fifty years before Giotto, the windows of Chartres, the mosaics of the baptistery in Florence, obviously represented individuals, but they did not attempt to resemble them: their style separated them from nature, which was primarily the world of men, so that they might become a part of the world of the cathedral or the baptistery, which was the world of God. In the sixteenth century, the religious scene was no longer related to the House of God, but to nature; the forms of art were no longer related to a transcendence, except to the extent that it was in accord with the testimony of our senses. Painting having become the major art, nature became so completely its field of reference that, for more than three centuries, Europeans could not conceive of a true art form that was not subject to it. Not the woods and the fields, because the landscape came into being relatively late; even less that cosmic, close-knit nature of mountains and waters, forests and beasts, whose serene or quivering symbols were boldly established in the painting of the Far East; not exactly a model, but a "realm of truth," which was claimed by both a realism that considered itself bound to it, and an idealization that considered it as its natural foundation (as did Molière and Racine). Those who disdained the mortal inhabitants of this pictorial nature conceived of Hades and the Elysian fields only in terms of nature's limits: nature became the invincible "unison" copied by Western artists even when they employed it in the service of the dream, the common realm in which Poussin and Goya, and all of the warring brothers of Europe, are reunited when we confront them with any Romanesque, Byzantine, or Far Eastern work—when we confront them with the masterpieces of all the painting of the world except their own. The common realm, the museum, in which a Courbet figure is sister to a Van Eyck figure, and even to Leonardo, but not to the *Theodora* in Ravenna.

The triumph of this reference to nature would have been sufficient to relegate all of the sacred art of Christianity to the limbo of incompetence or of pious reverence. The word "nature," always burdened with superimposed meanings, acquired new heights of prestige after the eighteenth century: it provided the only common point of reference for the works assembled in the museum prior to the time when the development of the landscape reached its apogee in Impressionism. The first annexations of the museum from realms beyond its own, notably that of the Primitives, not only raised no questions concerning this reference point: they confirmed it. To Vasari, Giotto's genius had been his substitution of nature for convention, and many people admired in Gothic art its diversion from the Romanesque convention, just as Vasari had admired in Giotto his diversion from the Byzantine convention. The presumption of incompetence, convincing enough when it was applied to the works of barbaric or "vandal" minds, was less so when applied to empires that had built the greatest monuments in the world, and whose sculptors and jewelers possessed conspicuous ability. But since a rigid frontalism, a full-face eye in a profiled head, are not in accord with the testimony of our senses, Egyptian art remained the greatest primitive art of humanity. The vast enterprise of idealization willed by antique sculpture to Italian painting, and representing to Europe the manifest summit of art, was inseparable from nature, from atmosphere, from shadow, from the "unison" from which it had fashioned fiction's most powerful tool. Nature was the stage on which the imaginary spectacles acknowledged by the testimony of our senses were played out, and this common theater assured the common point of reference acknowledged by works of art.

Great artists had always been conscious of a world distinct from that of the testimony of our senses, even though it might be only a secret world, and they knew that it formed a part of their own creation. This was true even of artists who were fully conscious of a specific power of color: Rubens, Rembrandt, and Watteau did not consider themselves simply purveyors of dreams, and Chardin did not think of himself as only a collector of jugs of wine. But even though none of the masters of the unreal had confused his work with its projection into the imaginary, all had permitted it. Corot, the contemporary of Ingres and of Delacroix, believed only in nature, which they claimed for their own, just as he did; Manet, who acknowledged the testimony of his senses only symbolically, defended *Olympia* in the name of the free interpretation of nature, which Cézanne would continue to extol.

The break would not be complete until the advent of cubism.

199

144. *School of the Mogols - The Emperor Tamerlane on His Throne (detail).*
145. *Rembrandt - The Emperor Tamerlane on His Throne.*

146. *Picasso - Portrait of Ambroise Vollard.*

The aesthetes of the end of the century preferred Botticelli's painting to Raphael's, *and* women who resembled the nymphs of *Primavera* to those who resembled the *Galatea* of the Villa Farnesina. Sarah Bernhardt thought she was portraying Byzantium, because her designers and decorators confused Byzantine art with anything that was pre-Botticelli. A two-dimensional art, even if it were the mosaics of Ravenna, might have an influence on style or on gestures—especially through a quality of affectation, as it is shown to us by Asia, from Persia to Japan, and by the mannerism of Gothic illuminations— but it did not dispose of the force brought to its canvases by the theater of Illusion. And even the mosaic is related to "nature," although distantly.

Rembrandt, when he seems to copy Indian miniatures, can make them a part of his art through the use of a few shadows, a few breaks in the continuous line of his model, a few allusions to depth; such an alteration becomes impracticable if we try to imagine replacing the Indian miniature with a *collage* by Braque. And while it is possible to prefer Botticelli's women to Raphael's, no one could prefer to Botticelli's women—or even to the women of the Ravenna mosaics or of Persian, Chinese, or Japanese paintings—women who would resemble the figures in cubist canvases. A cubist portrait may symbolically resemble its model (Picasso's *Vollard* and *Kahnweiler*, for example), but it does not allow us to imagine that model—especially in a form resembling the picture.

The enchantment of which painting had been the inexhaustible provider gave way before painting itself, while the museum without walls was opening to the figures and spectacles for which no part could be found in the opera then being played for Western audiences by the assemblage of masterpieces in the Louvre. To the prophets of Byzantium, the saints of the stained-glass windows, the gods of the Orient and of Asia, the African ancestor figures—all, like cubist paintings, strangers to illusionism—this assemblage could not offer the hospitality that the genius of Italy had offered to Rubens and Rembrandt. For nature unites art with the theater of illusion, while the sacred separates art from the testimony of our senses: Greek figures were admired because they resemble men, sacred figures because they do not resemble them. Little by little, reference to nature became one of the comic characteristics of the nonartist.

And so ceased the primacy of that nature which had mingled the countryside, the studio model, shadow, depth, truth, what we see, what we know, our most attentive observation and our most singular dreams; the atmosphere

202

147. *Leonardo da Vinci - St. John the Baptist (detail).*

148. *Torcello - Head of a Young Saint.* ▶

149. *Velazquez - Las Meninas.*

150. *Picasso - Las Meninas.*

in which the work of art had lived for several centuries, as it had lived for thousands of years in the shadow of the sacred place. But this "unison" was the area of relationship between man and the cosmos; the Western museum had been the museum of that relationship. The figures that were coming back to life, or that we were inheriting from heterogeneous civilizations, had not been subordinated to this nature. They could not penetrate its domain; but, in alliance with works of modern art, they could destroy it, as they were about to destroy the shadows of Velazquez, the shadow that was born with Leonardo and that died with Courbet.

It goes without saying that the vast metamorphosis which had transformed a will to express the supernatural into a clumsy approach to the imitation of nature—establishing nature as judge of the supernatural, and thereby erasing a thousand years of Christian art—was inseparable from a metamorphosis in the manner of seeing. The creation of every great art is inseparable from such a metamorphosis, which does not properly belong in the realm of vision, but of attention, and of a sort of projection toward the work, which leads the spectator to *recognize* in it what he expects from it, be it fetish or statue.

The little, time-formed rocks of Chinese collections, which are beginning to find a place in our museums, become works of art as a result of what the artist sees in them. But only a short time ago, we would not have looked

151. *Natural Rock.*

on them in this manner, any more than the twelfth century looked on Romanesque statues as works of art. But we do not look on a Virgin to whom we are praying in the same manner as we would observe the statue of a Virgin we admire as a personage or a painting of the Virgin we admire as a painting. At the beginning of this century, artists became acutely aware of this fact, which was summed up in Maurice Denis' famous phrase: "Before being a Virgin ... a picture is a flat surface covered with colors arranged in a certain order." And a sculpture is volume arranged in a certain order. By this, of course, he meant that we term picture, sculpture, work of art, and not God, divinity or crucifix, double or Black Virgin, whatever we look at in this manner. Maurice Denis knew very well that anyone who might have asserted to Giotto, to the master of the Avignon *Pietà*, to the sculptors of Chartres or of Rheims, that their Virgins were arrangements of color or volume *before* being Virgins, would have been accounted an idiot or a buffoon. To these artists, as to the devout masses of the people, color and volume were "arranged in a certain order" only to create Virgins.

Even Michelangelo would have said: "Volumes must be assembled in accordance with a certain order, *in order that* a Virgin may be worthy of representing the Mother of God." In his eyes sculpture and painting were still means to a manifestation of the divine; but the work was worthy of representing the Virgin Mother if it invoked prayer, *and* if it invoked admiration. The Egyptian effigy had been a double, the Romanesque Virgin a presence; Michelangelo's Virgin was a statue. And to him a statue of the Virgin must invoke admiration, just as the Romanesque masters had felt that it must invoke reverence. But this admiration might also be invoked by a profane figure: *Brutus*, *Leda*, or *Night*.

It was when Christianity chose its own means of expression from the forms created for the service of other gods that there began to emerge a value which challenged those supreme values it once had served. Neither the ancient East, nor the Middle Ages, had conceived of the idea we express in the word "art." The Greece of Pericles had not known of a work to express it. In order for this idea to be born, in order for papal Rome to be in a position to choose ancient Rome over Byzantium and the past of its own art over the art of Christendom's past; in order for a Christian to see in an Aphrodite a statue and not an idol, it was necessary that the works of artists be separated from the purpose that had given birth to them, from the function they had fulfilled, and even, at least in part, from the manner in which their creator had regarded them. The Renaissance suppressed the divinity of the gods it resurrected in

152. *Michelangelo - The Medici Madonna (detail).*

153. *Catalonia - Madonna and Child (detail).*

order to transform them into works of art—and this is what we are doing. But, the gods of Hellenistic or Roman antiquity had *also been* works of art,

154. *Mali - Masks.*

in the sense in which Florence understood the term, while the majority of the masterpieces we are resurrecting were created by artists for whom the idea of art did not exist.

The farther the range of our resurrections extends, the more obvious the metamorphosis becomes. Even if Michelangelo could believe that he might have looked on a statue by Lysippus with the same eyes with which it was regarded at the court of Alexander, or believe that in moving to the Vatican it had done no more than exchange one palace for another, neither Picasso nor Giacometti consider that they are looking at the masks in the *Musée de l'Homme* with the same eyes as the Africans for whom they were carved

and who watched them dance. We know that these masks were created for the dance and for music—for the ritual ceremony, movement, rhythm. The more we discover of the meaning of those arts that are united for us by their forms, the more we discover how widely divergent these meanings are. What common meaning exists between the erotic sculptures of India, the Sumerian statues, and the Romanesque saints? How could we admire each of them and all of them together, if it were not for the dazzling common metamorphosis which lights up the dark corners of their individual metamorphoses?

We still find it difficult to use the word "admire" without a feeling of uneasiness. The Renaissance truly admired antiques. But the emotion we experience before a Romanesque, Sumerian, or Aztec statue is not the emotion Michelangelo called admiration when he discovered the *Laocoön* or the Belvedere *Torso* in the Vatican.

Here we are touching on the metamorphosis of an emotion, which, for centuries, was one of the marks of distinction of a man of culture, into an emotion we no longer know how to name. If we call our museum without walls and the museum it is already summoning to take its place the "world of art," it is because we have no other term to describe it; just as we have no term to express the emotion it inspires in us. Having progressed from the Mediterranean to the globe itself, we still use for the globe the vocabulary of the Mediterranean. But Poussin's concept of an art of "delectation" ill fits the *Mothers* of Ellora, the Aztec *Goddess of Death*, Dogon masks, the Moissac *Vision of the Eternal*, the Perpignan "*Devout Christ*," the work of Goya, and even some Rembrandts. In our resurrection it is precisely this quality of delectation that has disappeared. And the world of the museum without walls is no more Michelangelo's world of admiration than was the world of reverence of the Romanesque sculptors.

When we consider the metamorphosis of the emotion inspired by works of art—which stems, to a very large degree, from their "surroundings"— we must again pause for a moment to think about their frames.

From the most completely transformed of Titian or Rembrandt portraits to the most mediocre portrait by Nattier, we can not regard an unframed figure without a sense of surprise: they seem amputated, altered. ( I remember the French and American curators, all of whom are familiar with the work of restoration, when they first saw the *Mona Lisa* unframed.) The religious "aura" of the framing of a retable has made us conscious of the Romanesque aura of secular framing. In each of its manifestations, from the small-scale    213

157. *Il Rosso - Love Chastised by Venus.*

architectural façades of the Renaissance, whose pilasters embellish and reduce the retable as the painting of the period embellishes and reduces faith; to the overpowering ropes of gilt that provide a link between paintings and the imagined catafalque, which is the obsession of Spain; to the profusion of flowery scrolls that seems to give life to, rather than ornament, the portraits of the daughters of the kings of France, the frame plays the part of mediator. Inevitably, it provides a link between the painting—which is always, somewhat obscurely, considered a part of the background—and the decorative arts of the palace, the home, or the apartment: it makes an *objet d'art* of the work of art. And it annexes it to the palace as Primaticcio's stuccoes annexed the frescoes of Il Rosso to the palace of Fontainebleau: bringing to mural painting not only a background, but also the accompaniment that once had been brought to it by the church. But we still find the frame hanging against the naked walls of modern museums. It no longer seems to provide a link between the picture and the background of a wall, which provides none, but it does suggest this background, return the scene it pictures to the time of the artist who painted it. Nevertheless, whether we see a Titian portrait in a Venetian palace, in the Pitti Palace, or in the most geometric of modern galleries, how can we fail to see that its lacework frame links it more with

158. *Nattier - Madame Adelaide Tying Knots.*

159. *Nattier - Madame Adelaide Tying Knots.*

160. *Veronese - Feast in the House of Simon.*

the unreal than with any time or place? The symbolists spoke of certain portraits as nude figures in dormant water; this suggestion of a profound mirror is inseparable from the use of frames, which also encircle mirrors, but the comparison would lose all relevance if it evoked a hand mirror, and it is not applicable to the scroll portraits of the Far East or to those in frescoes. At the time when it lost its religious character, the secular frame provided the link between the work and the unreal that the frame of the retable had once provided between the religious work and the supernatural. The execution of every court portrait, from Titian to Gainsborough, was influenced by the frame in which it would be set, just as the execution of a stained-glass window was influenced by the cathedral for which it was destined. The real portrait of Madame Adelaide is the temporal edifice that frames her likeness.

But if it is not surprising that a portrait of a doge of Venice seems to call for a frame in the style of his great, gilded gondola, or that the painted columns in the *Feast in the House of Simon* echo the real columns of the

217

*Salon d'Hercule* at Versailles, created by Mansart for the glorification of Veronese's painting, or that portraits of the Daughters of France should have been conceived as elements of stonework, is it also natural that paintings of the poor and wretched, of windmills, of wine jugs and of laborers, should not have resulted in the frameless picture toward which modern art is tending?

We are disturbed at the thought of Courbet framing his pictures in the style of the façade of the Paris Opera, when he saw them every day, in his studio, without a frame. Even though Giotto never saw his Scrovegni frescoes except on the walls of that chapel, and even though Van Eyck was more directly concerned with a portion of a retable than with a figure of *Eve*, all artists have, for centuries, known one place where frames play no part, even if they can be found there: their studio. But the artist himself considered the unframed picture unfinished—because the traditional secular frame came into being at the same time as the primacy of "nature," a by-product of the essential ambiguity of Western illusionism. *Trompe l'œil* having never been more than a game, painting was expected to compete with actual appearance without becoming lost in it; to belong to both the realm of appearance *and* to another realm, which, when it was no longer that of idealization became

161. *Braque - Seascape.*

that of "painting" as such. The frame, which had contributed so much to the transformation of women into Venus, of models into portraits, contributed no less to the transformation of pitchers into still lifes.

With the advent of Impressionism, painters began to find it increasingly difficult to reconcile their work with frames. The curators of museums have found it even more difficult, and now enclose the Van Goghs in Amsterdam in slender strips of wood or imbed the Monets of the Louvre in the wall, to free them from the Louis XV or Second Empire confections which once framed them, and whose use for this purpose becomes incomprehensible if we forget that they were attempting, ingenuously, to provide a link between modern painting and ancient rooms. Braque and Rouault sometimes painted their own frames, thereby making them into an annex to the picture; a reversal of the practices of the past, which tends only to isolate the painting while concealing its basic framework—something that could be accomplished by the most inconspicuous strip of wood, when the wall is white and unbroken. And the museum, which has itself become white, displays some selected older works in this manner. Carpaccio would be troubled by the metamorphosis of his *Courtesans*. This is why it is very surprising that we have not noticed that we are presently engaged in developing a world of art from which *all* frames have disappeared: the world of art books. In them the frame is replaced by the margin of the page. For a picture without some form of border irritates us, even though we accept the fresco *or the detail*. This margin, inherited from engraving and from reproduction (but reproductions were often destined to be framed), is also formed by the white walls of present-day museums and galleries; this unframed old canvas is *Burgomaster Six* as we would have seen it in Rembrandt's studio, *Isabelle of Portugal* in Titian's, the *Mona Lisa* in Leonardo's. But Rembrandt, Titian, and Leonardo knew that they were painting fetishes of the unreal, as a Romanesque sculptor knew that he was carving a Virgin, and as an African sculptor knows that he is carving an ancestor. The suppression of frames is revealing: what has disappeared from the art book, along with the frame of the retable, is the church, but also the Christian world in which the picture had its existence, the sanctuary for which it was created; what has disappeared with the secular frame is the palace, but also the world of the unreal in which the picture had its existence, and for which it was created. The common reference to nature had masked these private worlds in which the successive forms of art were developed —and the abandonment of this reference reveals the secret presence of a new "unison" in which their metamorphosis brings them together.

To say that the saints, the Danaës, the faces of the poor, and the pitchers of water or of wine have become paintings, that the gods and the ancestors have become sculpture, is to say that all of these figures have deserted the world in which they were created for our world of art (which is not only the world of *our* art); that our museum without walls is founded on the metamorphosis of the surroundings of the works it includes. It is an ignorance of this metamorphosis that so often causes museums to be qualified as cemeteries. The life lost by works of art when they entered the museum was precisely their surroundings in the sanctuary or the palace; this is why so many museums are still palaces, and why the Louvre cannot shelter African art. The paintings gathered in the museums of America have been described, a trifle hastily, as "fish out of water," but those who described them were forgetting that this metamorphosis has led more of the fish to immortality than to death. The curators of museums will not much longer be content with "the best possible presentation of objects": even now they are seeking a means of expressing the mysterious unity of works of art, of which they are constantly reminded by the images in books published by the museums themselves. The great Venetians have lost their frame and their palace? The Far Eastern wash drawing has lost its scroll, the illumination has lost its book, and we term a few pebble mosaics, some fragments of vases and potsherds "Greek painting." Technically, it was not impossible for Titian's *Charles V* to retain its frame in books; or for vases to retain their forms. But frame, vase, palace, or sanctuary separated images from the common language spoken in the assembly of arts of the past. The vast area of the museum without walls that reassembles pictures and statues is orienting the transformation of the real museums by a process of intellectualization unprecedented in art, and by its destruction of surroundings.

A great many minor metamorphoses converge into a fundamental metamorphosis that has led to the birth of our world of art. If an African sculpture, in our museums, is no longer the mask of a ritual dance that it was originally, a statue in the grottoes of China, which has never been moved and which we may never see, is no longer what it was just half a century ago. The everyday succession of discoveries has sufficed to alter our concept of great styles. The Chinese style was one of curios, and then one of Buddhist grottoes and Sung painting, and it has changed since the appearance of T'ang frescoes, the painting of "individualists" and eccentrics, the bronzes of the great dynasties; since the mask in the Art Institute of Chicago has come to
220   be considered one of the major examples of Chinese art, the figures of Lung-

163. *Botticelli - Venus and Mars.*

men, confronted with it, freed of grotesque elements and separated from their statue-columns, no longer have the same intensity.

We term "styles" the expressions of civilizations through forms, but we use the same term, more modestly, for groupings of forms. The succession of discoveries, the museum without walls, the thinking of art historians join together to shatter the foundations of these groupings, as we have learned from the sudden appearance of Sumerian art, of the earliest Gothic art (which had previously been considered Romanesque), of mannerism. And a great many works are modified by a change in their family relationship, as if they had lost their "appurtenance of style." Our present relationship to the painting of the Quattrocento is a good example of this. This painting remains bound to Vasari's outline of it, even though we no longer attach any great importance to Vasari himself: a reconquest of the dialogue with antiquity, won by Florentine genius over the style of Byzantium and of the regions beyond the Alps. All of the museums had been developed in accordance with this view. But if we accept the view of the last masters of the history of Italian painting, and make of Padua, and not Florence, the chosen city of the humanists of the second half of the century; if we grant to Squarcione's studio an influence equal to that of Masaccio's frescoes, we will see—in the museum without walls at first, in exhibitions later, and finally in the real museums—gathered together as a style, works that until that time were scattered, considered minor, or linked in our minds to different styles. Even if this historical perspective does not convince us, it is not only Paduan paintings that appear in a new light, it is also those of Ferrara, of Mantua, of eastern

Italy, a whole family of works whose chromatic intensity leads us directly to that which united the Venetians of the first quarter of the sixteenth century and their *German* contemporaries, Grünewald and Altdorfer; works which cause us to change our views of the rocky glitter of Mantegna, the knotty arabesque of the last Botticellis. Every major confrontation also calls for a metamorphosis in our manner of seeing, especially when pictures are no longer competing with imaginary spectacles: the emotions we experience on viewing Botticelli's *Primavera* are not the same, if we are remembering the frescoes in the Palazzo Schifanoia in Ferrara, as they would be if we are thinking of Raphael's *Galatea* in Rome.

Our recognition that the mere creation of every great art modifies those

164. *Ercole de' Roberti - The Loves of Venus and Mars (detail).*

that preceded it has made us all the more sensitive to the fluidity of the past. After Van Gogh, Rembrandt is no longer altogether what he was after Delacroix. When Uccello takes his place in the front ranks, Guercino disappears. (How can we be interested in Guercino? Perhaps as Velazquez was, when he bought his paintings for the king of Spain.) Our Uccello is obviously neither what he considered himself nor what the eighteenth century considered him; and our Guercino is no more so. The museum style, created by the accumulation of protective varnishes, bound Titian and Tintoretto together to the point of absurdity—until the time when cleaning freed them from an uncomfortable fraternity. When did the varnish of museums become intolerable to their curators, if not when painting itself became clear? Every resurrection projects on the past its sudden beam of light and vast patches of shadow; it has not been a very long time since Piero della Francesca came to be considered one of the greatest painters in the world, but since he has, Raphael has greatly changed.

An art, in the eyes of its contemporaries, lives by what it creates, but also by what it has created: by the arts of the future, which it seems to carry within itself, and which the years will limit to the art that takes its place. But even though metamorphosis causes it to lose both its accent of discovery and the plurality of its promises, the creation that orients its future also recomposes for it a past. Who was it, for example, who brought antique sculptures back into the light; searchers in the rubble of the past, or the masters of the Renaissance who looked on them and recognized what they saw? Who, if not Florence, silenced the Gothic artists? The destiny of Phidias was in the hands of Michelangelo, who never saw his statues: the austere genius of Cézanne glorified the luxuriant Venetians who were Michelangelo's despair, and affixed a seal of brotherhood to the painting of El Greco. It was the stumps of candles planted in the brim of his straw hat by the mad Van Gogh, while he painted the café in Arles at night, that provided the light for Grünewald's return. Turn-of-the-century frock coats of the Café Guerbois, ghosts of the Café de la Coupole! The revolt against appearances, becoming ever more effective as it progresses from the studios of the rue des Batignolles to the Bateau-Lavoir, is answered by the resurrection, in history's bloodiest century, of all the arts of the earth.... Metamorphosis is not an accident, it is the very life of the work of art.

It is this realization that is the origin of the feeling of metamorphosis *taking place*, which we experience in our relation with the museum without walls and, less directly, with our great real museums. Both of these have changed greatly since this book was first published. The word "Cubism" has ceased to be a derisive label for a major revolution: Kandinsky, Klee, and Mondrian are now united with Braque and Picasso, with Léger and Gris, in a realm that is foreign to theories, and even to schools, since the School of Paris will be only the continuation of the masters of modern painting: this realm is that of the proclamation of the rights of autocracy in painting, of the discovery that creation, in art, can become as *contagious* as "beauty." The conflict between representational and nonrepresentational painters is of importance only because of the prize it carried, which was the freedom of the artist (Pollock begins with *Olympia*), even if this were simply the freedom to find new means of representation. It will be a good while before it is abandoned. In museums of modern art, the art that is considered precursory is no longer that produced by the Impressionist revolution: it is all art that rebels against submission to spectacle. The art of today—the first that is not subject to either the sacred, as was the art of the East, or the divine, as was the art of Greece, or Christ, as was medieval art, or to the unreal, or to realism—continues to explore the art of the past; and for that art the "time of the finite world" has not begun. It was only yesterday that we discovered the lintel of the abbey church at Cluny, the mosaics of Pella, the real frescoes of Fontainebleau, the Palenque heads, Han-yang vases, Luristan bronzes, pre-Buddhist Japanese art, Parthian statues, Sao terra cottas, the Lascaux cave paintings, the rupestral art of the Sahara. The great museum of African art does not yet exist.

On the other hand, the magnificent chaos of yesterday's discoveries is gradually assuming its shape and form. The masters of Avignon and of Nouans, Piero della Francesca, Georges de Latour, Uccello, Masaccio, Cosimo Tura, Breughel, Le Nain, Vermeer, Chardin, Goya *(The Duchess of Alba* was sold for seven guineas around 1850), Daumier—some of these have been revealed to us for the first time, while others have taken or resumed their rightful place. The individualism of the nineteenth century prepared the welcome given to a many-faceted past whose forgotten styles are reappearing in a less disorganized fashion than that in which the artists themselves have reappeared. Their procession revives the conflict between spiritualization and idealization, eternity and immortality. Diana, the nymph, and Venus are answered by the Mesopotamian divinities, *Queen Nefretete*, *The Visitation* of Chartres and of Rheims, the Bamberg *Eve*, *The Lady Donors* of Naumburg; the genius of the Romanesque churches, called forth by the genius of a Cézanne, who was scarcely aware of it, and served by photography and the    225

165. *Greek Art - The Koré of Euthydikos.*

museum, now fraternizes with the genius of archaic Greece, of Buddhist China, and of India; summoning back to life its own ancestors, from Rheims to Chartres and from Chartres to Moissac, from Bamberg to Compostella, and to all of pre-Romanesque sculpture and the art of the great migrations, it sheds light on the genius of Mexico, of the Iberians, of Sumer, and finally on that of the Negro and of prehistory. The word "primitives," which first was used to designate the painters of the fourteenth century, today designates the painters of the caverns, and the sculptors of Oceania.

All of this resurrection, which had its birth in Europe, has only one precedent, and that too is European: the Renaissance. And it began as a violent Counter-Renaissance. But how can it be limited to the rejection of idealiza-

166. *Tenayuca (Mexico) - Head of a Serpent of the Sun.* ▶

167. *Art dogon - Statuette.*

168. *Beauvais - Head of a King.* ▶

169. *Picasso - The Reaper.*

tion, which seemed its original guiding force? At the very time that it opposed the severe style to the traditional style of antiquity, the *Koré of Euthydikos* to the *Medici Venus*, it discovered a "severe style" of Italy, from Masaccio to Piero della Francesca, it chose as its own a severe style of humanity in which Georges de Latour joins with Piero, a style whose breadth and rejection of allurement linked Giotto, El Greco, and Takanobu with the Greek archaics and with something that resembles them in China, in the ancient East, in Christendom; the *Koré of Euthydikos* and the *Queen Nefretete, The Charioteer* of Delphi and *The Kings* of Chartres. The resurrection also discovered a purity of color that allies itself to this denuded style in the simplicity of its approach, in the immobility of the figures, and in the perfection of the harmony: Corot, Chardin, Vermeer, the small paintings of Piero della Francesca. At the other pole, Grünewald, Altdorfer, and the German chromatism of the beginning of the sixteenth century, the irruption of Venice, some of the landscapes of Rubens, and then the stridency, the vast medley of colors that leads to the painted sculpture of the New Hebrides. Beyond the exaltation of color, the form that seems born of a struggle with all forms; Gallic coins, the fiber mask of New Britain, the twisted mask of the Eskimo shamans, the hieroglyphic head of Mexico.

This dialogue of the severe style of humanity with India, Africa, Sumerian *Fertilities*, and the forms of night, this dialogue that was ignored or rejected by all other civilizations, and born with us, is being carried on in a world that was also born with us: the world in which each masterpiece is supported by the testimony of all others, and becomes a masterpiece of a universal art whose values, still unknown, are even now being created by the assemblage of all of its works. A major work of Byzantine art is not only a *Prophet* more perfect than its rivals, even on a purely spiritual level, it is also a work worthy of all those we admire. Even if we know what major works owe to the circumstances of their birth, they come to us, through metamorphosis, as *fellows;* and in many respects the world of art that has replaced for us the primacy of nature is the world in which a *Siva* of Ellora is both a god of India and the fellow of *The Charioteer* of Delphi, of the *Eagle-Knight* of Mexico, of a statue-column, of Michelangelo's *Night*, of Rodin's *Balzac*, of an African mask. It is the world in which these images speak a different language, and the same language: a language of statues and a language of sculptures. And in this world that metamorphosis substitutes simultaneously for those of the sacred, of faith, of the unreal or the real, the new sphere of reference of artists is the museum without walls of each of them; 231

the new sphere of reference of art is the museum without walls of all.

If the picture that once was a panel is no longer related to its retable, or to its church, or even to its realm of the supernatural, and if it has ceased to be related to nature, it is related to the totality of known works, both originals and reproductions. But if an album devoted to the Louvre is deemed to reproduce the Louvre (and it would claim to reproduce only the master-pieces, which is a somewhat different matter, since the Louvre of 1956 was governed by history, and perhaps its masterpieces are governed by the obscure concept of the masterpiece) the totality of albums and other works devoted to art does not reproduce a museum that does not exist: it suggests it—and, more strictly, it constitutes it. It is not the testimonial or the souvenir of a place, like the album devoted to the cathedral of Chartres, the Uffizi, or Versailles: it creates an imaginary place that has no existence outside of its pages.

The broadest realm of images humanity has known is calling forth its sanctuary, as the realm of the supernatural called forth the cathedral. But this realm, which makes an island of any Louvre, however vast, is bringing back the faithful to all the Louvres, because their faith is the same. For phonograph records have not destroyed concerts; because we feel a need to rediscover the particular perfection or the irreplaceable texture of flesh, the real or imagined soul that belongs only to the original; because the dialogue between the Avignon *Pietà* and Titian's *Nymph and Shepherd* is not of entirely the same nature as the dialogue between their reproductions. If not the museum, what then will be the sanctuary for the works of *our* art? The apart-ments of those who buy them? As a rule, we begin by not buying them; and there is a great deal to be said regarding the harmony between Cézanne's *Grandes Baigneuses* or Picasso's *Guernica* and any living room, however "modern." Every painter hopes that, within a century or two, his canvases will be in museums. The respect inspired by art in a constantly increasing number of men separates it from the idea of private possession, and makes of the collector a temporary possessor. Even for ancient works, the private collection is the antechamber of the museum, and in Europe, as in Japan and America, the great collections, less and less often handed down and more and more often bequeathed, will at last come here. They will come to a museum that is seeking its form, and will undoubtedly be as different from ours as ours is from the galleries of the past. And it may not find this form until it has ceased confusing the work of art with the *objet d'art*, until it has learned from the museum without walls that its most profound influence is based on its relationship with death.

The museum is governed by history, and our conception of creation cannot entirely discount the historical succession of works. It seems, in fact, to be playing the role in the museum that once was played by nature. Considered as an object of history, the *Mona Lisa* is located between Verrocchio and Raphael, and she is a fellow to Alexander, of whom nothing remains but the glory and the transformation he imposed on the ancient world: Alexander is a dazzling moment of death. But *Mona Lisa* (or any major work) is not dead, even though she was born between Verrocchio and Raphael: it is Lisa del Gioconda who is dead. *Mona Lisa* is of her time, and outside of time. Our reaction to her is not on the level of knowledge but of *presence*. To love painting is, above all, to feel that this presence is radically different from that of the most beautiful piece of furniture of the same period; it is to know that a painting—the *Mona Lisa*, the Avignon *Pietà*, or Vermeer's *Young Girl with a Turban*—is not an object, but a voice. Such a presence, which is not possessed by Alexander, but is by a saint to *whom one prays*, is properly a part of survival, and belongs to life. Not to knowledge: to life. With the exception of supernatural presences, it is the only one that belongs to it. India, which still speaks to us, is profoundly enough separated from us to make us certain that we do not hear ancient Egypt, which can no longer speak to us; to affirm the fact that vanished civilizations or cultures—whatever name one gives to the varying forms the human adventure has assumed—have vanished forever. The soul of Sumer, of the kingdoms of the Andes or of the Gulf of Mexico, the soul of ancient Egypt are forever dead. The relationship of a priest of Isis and of an Egyptian sculptor—or even that of an Egyptian peasant—with the universe, is not comprehensible to us; and of what importance is it to know an emotion, and even more a faith, we have never experienced? Are we altogether certain of rediscovering the soul of the temples of Ellora, whose civilization has not vanished; of the Greek temples, from which our civilization claims descent; of the cathedrals, whose civilization is our own? If the soul of a civilization is linked to its fundamental relationship with the universe, it is not too much to say that, in essential matters, the world is a world of oblivion. But the major works of vanished civilizations, even the statues of the Pharaohs, the ophidian statues of the darkness of Sumer, the prehistoric beasts of caves, all of these figures that, only yesterday, *were still a part* of the kingdoms of oblivion, are alive to us, or carry within themselves the seed of their resurrection. The vast, wind-blown movement of clouds that sweeps civilizations on to death, and which blots out, one after another, the stars of Chaldea and the Star of the Shepherds, seems today to be passing in vain across the first constellation of images.... If not the eternity demanded for their works by the sculptors of Sumer and of Babylon, the immortality demanded for theirs by Phidias and Michelangelo, the museum without walls brings at least an enigmatic release from time to all the works of art it selects. And if it brings into being a Louvre crowded with the faithful, and never deserted, it is because the real museum is the presence, in life, of those things that should belong to death.

But we have discovered that resurrected works are not necessarily immortal. And that, if death cannot still the voice of genius, it is not because genius prevails over death by perpetuating the language of its beginnings, but by imposing a language that is constantly modified, sometimes forgotten, like an echo replying to the centuries in their own successive voices: the masterpiece does not sustain an infallible monologue, it imposes the intermittent and invincible dialogue of resurrections.

And in doing so, it moves along paths we cannot pick out, shrouded in the mists of an always transitory unison, of a museum without walls involved with its own progression, of an evolution in the art of the artists of today, of a metamorphosis that, daily and inexorably, changes the present into the past. The polychrome reconstructions of Munich attempted to restore life to Greece because it was considered unfitting that her works should come to the museums as corpses; but the waxworks museum, offered as a substitute for these corpses, was far from a rediscovery of their unconquerable fertility. A Romanesque cloister may be reconstructed in New York, an Egyptian mastaba in the Louvre, a Babylonian gate in Berlin, but their exile, their presence in a museum suffices to transform them into works of art. And even the portals of Chartres cannot entirely exempt their statues from metamorphosis, since these statues, to artists, are more closely related to those of the museum than to those of the ordinary neighborhood church; and as soon as the divine service is completed, the cathedrals become the largest galleries of the museum without walls. In 1910 it was generally thought the *Victory of Samothrace*, restored, would have regained her gold, her arms, and her trumpet. Without gold, without arms, and without trumpet, she has regained her prow of stone, and crowns the great staircase of the Louvre like a herald of the dawn: it is not toward Samothrace or Alexandria that we have set her flight, it is toward an exemplary Acropolis. Works of art are restored to life in our world of art, not in their own.

Greece did not change when the whole range of its works—from the severe figures to the geometric figures—became familiar to us, when we discarded

so many major works of Hellenistic art, through indifference, while admiring the *Victory of Samothrace* to such an extent that we made of it one of the most renowned statues in the world: the symbolic image suggested by the words "Grecian style" changed when this image no longer referred to an exemplary idealization that was considered the supreme expression of all art. The symbolic image of Byzantine art changes according to whether we see in it the interpretation of personages through a hieratic expressionism or the accession of a supernatural world to the realm of the Pantocrator; the image of African art changes according to whether we see in it the interpretation of personages through a savage expressionism or a magical creation; the image of the greatest art of India changes according to whether we see in it a fantastic expressionism or an attempt to reveal the Absolute through symbols. But if the demon of knowledge is right in leading us to understand the thinking of the India of yesterday, or the thinking of the Africa of today; if it is preferable to regard a Negro mask with an awareness of its "primordial force," rather than to consider it as a kind of savage Romanesque, it remains true that the primordial force provides only the same degree of access to African art as the great Christian texts provide for the tympanum of Moissac. The most knowledgeable student of prehistory is not necessarily the most convincing interpreter of the art of the caves; the wisest Egyptologist is not the one who is best at stimulating in us a love of Egyptian art. (And in the realm of art, of what use is an interpreter who enables us to understand an art he does not make us love?) If we were to rediscover, in front of one of the statues of Ellora, the emotion experienced by the first Hindus who saw it, we would rediscover their reverence and not simply an intensification of the emotion inspired in us by the statue. And we cannot rediscover *the* lost faiths, because *each of them* was truth.

But our civilization itself becomes a disturbing interpreter, since beauty is no longer anything more than one realm of art among others. The awkwardness attributed to medieval art, and to the arts of the ancient East, was not considered similar to that of a bad eighteenth-century painter; but for that matter, the portraits done by wandering painters, and the votive offerings of craftsmen, did not resemble the portraits and the Virgins of the Middle Ages. Gothic sculptors and painters were awkward because the best artists of the Dark Ages were necessarily naïve. But, for almost two centuries after the triumph of the Age of Enlightenment, religion was *also* considered naïve. Only Renan dared speak of "the religious nullity of the West," and he would have provoked laughter from Stendhal as well as from Voltaire, to whom

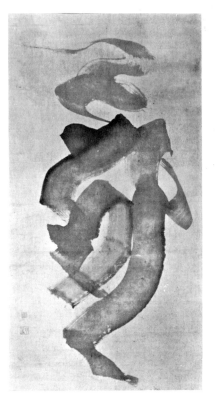

171. *Japanese Art - Hakuin - the Letter* "A."

religion could only mean deism, superstition, or imposture, and to whom the sacred was not conceivable. The images of the sacred are more immediate to us than the realm of the sacrosanct they made manifest, but we are aware of its existence—and of the existence of a nocturnal life of the soul more complex than evil itself. Is there less difference between a Greek or a Sumerian statue than there is between the idea of man proclaimed by Voltaire and that proposed by Freud?

The museum without walls is not a heritage of vanished ardors, it is an assemblage of works of art—but how can we see in these works only the expression of a will to art? A Romanesque crucifix is not a brother to a crucifix painted today by a talented atheist—which would express only his talent. It is a sculpture, but it is also a crucifix. We know little of what creates the "aura" surrounding a Sumerian statue, but we know very well that it never surrounds a modern sculpture. The Moissac *Eternal* does not affect us only through the order of its volumes, and we find in it the light of the countenance of the Father, just as we find the light of Christ in the tympanum of Autun, and in the humblest of Fra Angelico's paintings. For it is there. Titian lost his demiurgic power, but no Renoir, no Delacroix has painted the sister of his *Danaë*. Among all the calligraphic symbols of the Far East, the one chosen by our painters and our critics, with no knowledge of its significance, is the Hakuin character that expresses the beginning. In a world from which even the name of Christ had disappeared, a statue from Chartres would still be a statue; and if, in this civilization, this statue had not become invisible, the obscure significance it would express would not be the same as that of a statue by Rodin. What language is spoken by the pre-Columbians, of whom we still know so little, by Gallic coins, by the bronzes of the steppes, cast by tribes of whom we know nothing at all? What language is spoken by the bisons of the caves?

The languages of art are not similar to the spoken word, but are secret brothers to music. (For different reasons than those that might have been presumed when painting rejected imitation; considered only as languages, not as an arbitrary expression of freedom.) We know what separates every work of art from the ideology that gave it birth or that justifies it. What is said to us by *The Night Watch*, the last Titians and the *Montagne Sainte-Victoire*, *The Thinker*, the tympanum of Moissac, the statue of Prince Gudea and that of the Pharaoh Zoser, the African *Ancestor*, can be said only by forms, just as what is said to us by Palestrina's *Kyrie*, by *Orfeo*, *Don Giovanni* or the Ninth Symphony can be said only by notes of a scale. There is no translation.

It is what is said *to us* by these sculptures and these paintings, and not what they have said. Undoubtedly, what is said to us by the figures of the Royal Portal has its origins in what they once said to the people of Chartres, and is very different from what is said to us by the statues of Siva. But, even if the idea of art was foreign to them, the sculptors of genius who carved these statues wanted to create figures more worthy of reverence than those

◀ 172. *Elephanta (India) - Mahesamurti (detail).*

that preceded them, and to which they compared them, deliberately or not—as the faithful did, instinctively. When the *Kings* were no longer compared to their own ancestors, but to antique statues, their voice was stilled. And if, after so many years of oblivion, we hear the song that follows after a plainsong of a crusade or a chant of the *Ramayana*, it is not because the historians have restored the text to us, or because we have rediscovered the faith of the twelfth century or of the age of the Vedas; it is because we admire them in the company of the statues of Sumer and of the Indian grottoes, of the Acropolis and of the tombs of Florence—in the company of all the statues of the earth. It is the song of metamorphosis, and no one before us has heard it— the song in which esthetics, dreams, and even religions are no longer more than librettos to an inexhaustible music.

# ANALYTICAL INDEX

to Delacroix, Constable, Valenciennes, Corot - Conflict with "finish" — p. 58 - Sketch or picture? — p. 61 - The adventure of Impressionist ideology - Impressions; interpretations not governed by imitation - Theory and practice — p. 65 - Art tends toward an annexation of the world - *The Chair*, Van Gogh's ideogram - The importance of the subject diminishes - Primacy of the landscape and the still life — p. 66 - *Painting itself* - Supreme value for modern painters - Rembrandt and Goya, precursors of an outcast art — p. 67 - The nineteenth - century artist breaks with four thousand years of art — p. 68 - Spiritual union of artists, painters, poets, and musicians — p. 70 - Ostracism, source of fertility - "To paint like Poussin, after nature..." - New arts: Mesopotamia, Mexico — p. 70 - Forms dispensing with imitation — p. 71 - Japanese prints: an air of freedom - Byzantium — p. 72 - Another style, not another school — p. 73 to 76 - The cinema - Its means of reproduction, the photograph; its means of expression, the sequence of planes - The ideal medium for the expression of fiction.

## CHAPTER III

P. 77 - Reproduction — p. 78 - Italianism loses strength — p. 79 - Reproduction, a factor in changing viewpoints - Rubens' work — p. 80 - The album - The exhibition — p. 81 - Gothic art rediscovered — p. 82 - Interpretation of sculpture for reproduction in black and white - centering, lighting - works reproduced *lose their relative proportions* — p. 84 - The phenomenon of photographic enlargement creates fictitious arts — p. 88 to 96 - The role of reproduction in relation to the minor arts — p. 99 - Liberty of the artist revealed in ivories and in gold and silverware — p. 102 - The dialogue resulting from a comparison of photographs — p. 106 - The fragment is one of the great masters — p. 110 - New processes of printing, their possibilities — p. 111 - Reproduction does not compete, it suggests - The history of art, a history of that which can be photographed - Problems of color reproduction — p. 113 - The miniature — p. 114 - New relationship with the picture and the fresco — p. 120 - The civilization of the book — p. 125 - The Christian mosaic cannot enter the museum without undergoing a metamorphosis — p. 129 - The stained - glass window — p. 130 - Its color, a lyric expression - Monumental painting, in harmony with the cathedral, alive at every hour of the day — p. 134 - The rug — p. 136 - Tapestry, a kind of modern art — p. 139 - The fresco; its resurrection, from the West to Egypt and Japan - Different palettes — p. 146 - To Baudelaire, the sculpture of the Middle Ages was a "bastard art" - To the Romantics, the Middle Age was the fourteenth and fifteenth centuries: the Germany of horned devils - A Gothic art without a Romanesque art — p. 147 - The birth of modern art coincides with the destruction of the primacy of the antique — p. 148 - The end of the idea of ownership of the work of art frees it from its quality of *objet d'art* — p. 160 - Photography reveals the broadest artistic domain man has known - A heritage extended even further by retrospective exhibitions — p. 161 - Style, the legitimate expression of the creative intent — p. 162 - One of the major characteristics of art: the expression of the artist - The museum was an affirmation, the museum without walls is an interrogation.

## CHAPTER IV

P. 163 - The profound metamorphosis of works - The past has reached us without its colors — p. 165 - Greek statues have become white - The Romanesque world of color is now revealed in its frescoes - Patina and decay — p. 167 - The problem of repainted statues - Restoration — p. 168 - Mutilations have their style also — p. 171 - Greek art still occupies the place of honor, but not for the same works - The constant questioning of the nature of the universe — The end of the oriental fatalities — p. 174 - Greek figures; figures man would have chosen had he been God: the acanthus is what man would have made of the artichoke - Birth of the smile - The feminine nude — p. 178 - The techniques of Greece and those of Italy — p. 179 - Time has brought about a metamorphosis in the Antique of the museum - The gods are being resurrected without their divinity — p. 180 - Metamorphosis of the arts of the sacred: to Cézanne, a crucifix was a piece of sculpture - Painting as a means of expression of poetry — p. 181 - "Painting is poetry that *can be seen*" — p. 182 - Mannerism — p. 184 - The poetry of dreams - Baudelaire and Michelangelo — p. 188 - Painting creates its own poetry - Renoir, Chagall, Dufy find their specific poetry — p. 190 - 191 - Realist painting - The portrait does not escape its own time; it frees its model from time — p. 192 - The metamorphosis of a realist painting is less obvious than that of a statue — p. 194 - The Egyptian funerary statue is no longer anything if it ceases to be a *double* - The harmony between sculpture and the sacred place: Mesopotamia, Mexico; but less obvious for Gothic art — p. 195 - The frame of the retable — p. 197 - From the sixteenth to the nineteenth century, in painting, nature becomes synonymous with a "realm of truth" — p. 198 - The invincible "unison" of Western artists — p. 201 - Cubism breaks with nature — p. 201 - We cannot imagine the model for a cubist portrait in a form resembling the picture — p. 206 - The creation of a great art is inseparable from a metamorphosis in the manner of seeing — p. 207 - To Michelangelo, a statue of the Virgin must invoke prayer - The works of artists are separated from their function — p. 210 - African masks, created for the dance — p. 213 - Different meanings of the word "admire" - The secular frame — p. 219 - An unframed picture is unfinished - Impressionism and the frame — p. 219 - In art books, the frame is the margin — p. 220 - The museum without walls is orienting the transformation of the real museums - Styles; discoveries modify them — p. 222 - Raphael has changed since Piero della Francesca has come to be admired — p. 224 - 226 - The museum without walls and the real museum continue to change - The conflict between spiritualization and idealization - A "severe style" of humanity — p. 232 - Henceforth each masterpiece becomes a part of a universal art — p. 233 - The museum: all of the private collections will at last come here - Lisa del Gioconda is dead; the *Mona Lisa* is a voice, a presence — p. 234 - The museum without walls brings release from time - Its presence in a museum transforms a work into a work of art — p. 239- The languages of art are not similar to the spoken work, but are secret brothers to music.

THE ANALYTICAL INDEX AND THE ICONOGRAPHIC DOCUMENTATION OF THIS WORK WERE COMPILED BY MADELEINE DANY.

# ICONOGRAPHIC DOCUMENTATION

1. *Venice, Museo Correr, salla Carpaccio.* (Archivio fotografico, Direzione civici musei.)

2. TÉNIERS, DAVID II, *called* THE YOUNGER (1610-1690). The Archduke Leopold in His Gallery at Brussels *(detail). Around* 1647. *Signed. Madrid, the Prado.* 1,06 × 1,29 *m.* (Alinari.)

3. FILIPPO LIPPI (1406-1469). Madonna with Two Angels *(detail). Florence, the Uffizi. Wood. Dimensions of the whole :* 0,95 × 0,62 *m.* (Galerie de la Pléiade-Scala.)

4. LEONARDO DA VINCI (1452-1519). Portrait of the Mona Lisa, called La Gioconda *(detail). Paris, Musée du Louvre. Wood. Dimensions of the whole* 0,97 × 0,53 *m.* (Bulloz.)

5. GIAN LORENZO BERNINI (1598-1680). The Ecstasy of St. Theresa *(detail). Rome, Santa Maria della Vittoria, Cornaro Chapel (left transept). Marble. (*Alinari-Viollet.)

6. GIOTTO DI BONDONE (1266-1337). *Padua, Chapel of the Arena (Scrovegni chapel).* The Meeting of Joachim and Anne at the Golden Gate *(detail). Around* 1303-1305. In situ. *Mural painting.* (Alinari-Giraudon.)

7. GIULIO CESARE PROCACCINI (*ca* 1570-1625). The Penitent Magdalen and an Angel. *Milan, Pinacoteca della Brera. Canvas.* 1,37 × 0,97 *m.* (Scala.)

8. DOMINIQUE INGRES (1780-1867). Portrait of Louis-François Bertin, called Bertin the Elder. 1832. *Dated and signed. Paris, Musée du Louvre. Canvas.* 1,16 × 1,95 *m.* (Galerie de la Pléiade-Draeger.)

9. HONORÉ DAUMIER (1808-1879). Portrait of Gazan. 1835. *Paris Bibliothèque Nationale, Cabinet des Estampes. Lithograph.* 0,238 × 0,160 *m. Appeared in No* 245 *of* La Caricature, *July* 16, 1835, *plate* 510. (Galerie de la Pléiade-La Photothèque.)

10. REMBRANDT, HARMENSZ VAN RIJN (1606-1669). The Three Crosses. *Musée du Petit Palais (Duthuit Collection). Etching.* 0,387 × 0,451 *m.* (Galerie de la Pléiade-Draeger.)

11. MICHELANGELO BUONARROTI (1475-1564). Pietà Rondanini *(detail).* 1564. *Milan, Castello Sforzesco. Marble. Height:* 1,95 *m.* (Anderson-Giraudon.)

12. ROBUSTI, JACOPO, *called* IL TINTORETTO (1518-1594). St. Augustine Healing the Lepers. 1549-1550. *Vicenza, Civic Museum. Canvas.* 2,55 × 1,75 *m.* (Scala.)

13. BARTOLOMÉ ESTÉBAN MURILLO (1617-1682). Young Girl and Her Duenna. 1665-1675. *Washington, National Gallery of Art (Widener Collection). Canvas.* 1,25 × 1,05 *m.* (Museum.)

14. ÉDOUARD MANET (1832-1883). The Balcony. 1868-1869. *Signed. Paris, Musée du Jeu de Paume. Canvas.* 1,70 × 1,245 *m. The personages represented are friends of the painter: Berthe Morisot seated, Jenny Claus, and the painter Guillemet.* (Giraudon.)

15. DIEGO RODRIGUEZ VELAZQUEZ Y DE SILVA (1599-1660). The Infanta Donna Margarita of Austria *(detail). Around* 1660. *Madrid, the Prado. Canvas. Dimensions of the whole:* 2,12 × 1,47 *m.* (Galerie de la Pléiade-La Photothèque.)

16. FRANS HALS (*ca* 1580-1666). The Women Governors of the Almshouse at Haarlem *(detail).* 1664. *Haarlem, Frans Hals Museum. Canvas. Dimensions of the whole:* 1,705 × 2,485 *m. This painting has a counterpart:* The Governors of the St. Elizabeth Hospital at Haarlem. (Museum-Nico Zomer.)

17. ÉDOUARD MANET (1832-1883). Portrait of Clemenceau. *Around* 1879-1880. *Paris, Musée du Jeu de Paume. Canvas.* 0,94 × 0,74 *m.* (Giraudon.)

18. FRANCISCO JOSÉ DE GOYA Y LUCIENTES (1746-1828). The Burial of the Sardine. 1793. *Madrid, Real Academia de Bellas Artes de San Fernando. Wood.* 0, 83 × 0,62 *m.* (Galerie de la Pléiade-La Photothèque.)

19. HONORÉ DAUMIER (1808-1879). The Chess Players. *Around* 1863. *Signed. Paris, Musée du Petit Palais. Wood.* 0,24 × 0,32 *m.* (Bulloz.)

20. FRANCISCO JOSÉ DE GOYA Y LUCIENTES (1746-1828). The Shootings of May 3, 1808, *or* The Shootings of la Moncloa. 1814-1815. *Madrid, the Prado. Canvas.* 2,66 × 3,45 *m.* (Scala.)

21. ÉDOUARD MANET (1832-1883). The Execution of the Emperor Maximillian. *Manheim, Städistische Kunsthalle. Canvas.* 2,52 × 3,05 *m. This*

painting is signed and dated June 19, 1867, date of the execution, not of the work. (Gustav Schwarz.)

22. ÉDOUARD MANET (1832-1883). Olympia *(detail)*. 1863. *Dated and signed. Paris, Musée du Jeu de Paume. Canvas. Dimensions of the whole:* 1,30 × 1,90 m. (Giraudon.)

23. PAUL CÉZANNE (1839-1906). A Modern Olympia. *Around* 1873. *Paris, Musée du Jeu de Paume. Canvas.* 0,46 × 0,55 m. (Galerie de la Pléiade-Draeger.)

24. PAUL CÉZANNE (1839-1906). Still Life with Clock. 1869-1870. *Paris, private collection. Canvas.* 0,54 × 0,73 m. *Formerly in the collection of E. G. Robinson, Beverly Hills, California.* (Galerie de la Pléiade-La Photothèque.)

25. ÉDOUARD MANET (1832-1883). Study for the Bar des Folies-Bergère. *Finished in* 1881. *Amsterdam, Stedelijk Museum. Canvas.* 0,47 × 0,56 m. *The counter in the foreground is not in Manet's hand; it was added after his death. We do not know when or by whom. But in* 1912, *Meier-Graefe, in his book on Manet, reproduced the work intact.* (Museum.)

26. ALESSANDRO MAGNASCO (1667-1747). Convicts in Prison. *Between* 1711 *and* 1735. *Bordeaux, Musée des Beaux-Arts. Canvas.* 1,15 × 1,43 m. (Puytorac-P.-Y. Laplace.)

27. HONORÉ FRAGONARD (1732-1806). Portrait of the Abbot of Saint-Non, *still known under the name* Fantasy Figure. 1769. *Paris, Musée du Louvre. Canvas.* 0,80 × 0,65 m. *On the back of the canvas is written: "Portrait of M. l'abbé de Saint-Non painted by Fragonard in* 1769 *in one hour's time."* (Galerie de la Pléiade-Draeger.)

28. HENRI DE TOULOUSE-LAUTREC (1864-1901). Yvette Guilbert. *Private collection. Sketch.* (Galerie de la Pléiade.)

29. HENRI DE TOULOUSE-LAUTREC (1864-1901). Yvette Guilbert. 1894. *Albi Museum. Drawing; charcoal, heightened with thin oil colors, on coarse paper.* 1,86 × 0,93 m. (Galerie de la Pléiade-Draeger.)

30. PETER PAUL RUBENS (1577-1640). Philopoemen Recognized by an Old Lady. *Paris, Musée du Louvre. Wood.* 0,50 × 0,66 m. (Galerie de la Pléiade-Draeger.)

31. EUGÈNE DELACROIX (1798-1863). The Sultan of Morocco Mulay Abd er-Rahman Receiving the Count de Mornay, the French Ambassador. *Paris, private collection. Sketch. Canvas.* 0,31 × 0,40 m. (Galerie de la Pléiade-Draeger.)

32. PIERRE HENRI DE VALENCIENNES (1750-1819). Roof in Sunlight. *Paris, Musée du Louvre. Paper on cardboard.* 0,182 × 0,365 m. *On the back of this painting is written: "Loggia di Roma."* (National museums.)

33. EUGÈNE DELACROIX (1798-1863). The Battle of Taillebourg (the victor was St. Louis, July 21, 1242). 1837. *Signed and dated. Versailles, Galerie des Batailles. Canvas.* 4,85 × 5,55 m. (Bulloz.)

34. EUGÈNE DELACROIX (1798-1863). The Battle of Taillebourg. *Around* 1837. *Paris, Musée du Louvre. Sketch. Canvas* 0,53 × 0,66 m. (Giraudon.)

35. REMBRANDT, HARMENSZ VAN RIJN (1606-1669). The Company of Captain Frans Banninq Cocq *called* The Night Watch *(detail)*. 1642. *Dated and signed. Amsterdam, Rijksmuseum. Canvas. Present dimensions of the whole:* 3,59 × 4,38 m. *Original dimensions:* 3,87 × 5,02 m. *The painting was trimmed around* 1715 *for placement between two doorways in the town hall at Amsterdam.* (Museum.)

36. HONORÉ DAUMIER (1808-1879). Mother Holding Her Child. *Around* 1865-1870. *Signed. H. D. Zürich, private collection. Sketch. Canvas.* 0,39 × 0,32 m. (Walter Dräyer.)

37. EUGÈNE DELACROIX (1798-1863). Lion Hunt 1854. *Private collection. Sketch. Canvas.* 0,86 × 1,15 m. (Galerie de la Pléiade-Draeger.)

38. CLAUDE MONET (1840-1926). The Japanese Bridge. *Paris, private collection. Canvas.* 0,93 × 0,89 m. (Galerie de la Pléiade-Draeger.)

39. MAURICE DE VLAMINCK (1876-1958). Interior. 1903-1904. *Paris, Musée national d'Art moderne. Canvas.* 0,65 × 0,54 m. (Galerie de la Pléiade-La Photothèque.)

40. VINCENT VAN GOGH (1853-1890). The Chair and the Pipe (or The Yellow Chair. 1888-1889. *Signed Vincent. London, The Tate Gallery (Courtauld Collection). Canvas.* 0,93 × 0,735 m. (Museum.)

41. PETER PAUL RUBENS (1577-1640). Abraham's Sacrifice. *Paris, Musée du Louvre. Wood.* 0,50 × 0,65 m. (Galerie de la Pléiade-Draeger.)

42. *Early photography.* La Castiglione. (Galerie de la Pléiade.)

43. *Recent photography.* Dancer. (Galerie de la Pléiade.)

44. PETER PAUL RUBENS (1577-1640). Landscape with a Cart. *After* 1630. *Rotterdam, Boymans-Van Beuningen Museum. Wood.* 0,495 × 0,547 *m.* Museum.)

45. Iberian Art. The Lady of Elche. *Early photography.* 3$^d$ *or* 4th *century B.C. Madrid, The Prado. Limestone. Light traces of painting. Height:* 0,56 *m.* (Galerie de la Pléiade.)

46. Iberian Art. The Lady of Elche. *Recent photography.* (Tel-Vigneau.)

47. Mesopotamian Art (?). Goddess of Fertility· 3d *millennium B.C. Paris, private collection· Terra cotta. Height:* 0.125 *m.* (Roger Parry.)

48. Mesopotamian Art (?). Goddess of Fertility *(detail).* (Roger Parry.)

49. Statuette of a Steatopygic Woman. *Prehistoric. Cairo, Museum. Terra cotta. Height:* 0,17 *m.; from head to foot :* 0,25 *m. This statuette was found in a tomb at Aniba in the Sudan.* (Hassia.)

50. *Cyprus* (?). Female Musician *or* Woman Playing a Lute. *New Empire.* 19th-20th *dynasty. Cairo, Museum. Terra cotta. Height:* 0,21 *m.* (Hassia.)

51. *Cyprus* (?). Female Musician. *Profile.* (Hassia.)

52. Gallic Art. Coin of the Osismii *(detail):* Auriga (The Charioteer) stylized as a head. *Paris, Bibliothèque Nationale, Cabinet des Médailles. Gold. On the reverse side; a single horse.* (Ina Bandy.)

53. Japanese Art. *Tachibana-mura, Namekata-gun, Ibaragi-ken (northwest of Tokyo).* Haniwa *(funerary statuette)* Portraying a Monkey. *Period of the Great Sepulchres.* 5th-6th *century. Tokyo, private collection. Terra cotta, with traces of red pigment. Height:* 0,257 *m.* (Auskaen, Nara.)

54. Byzantine Art. Plaque from a *Gospel book. Lower section :* The Childhood of Bacchus *(detail):* Satyr and Maenad Dancing. 5th-6th *century. Paris, Bibliothèque Nationale, Cabinet des Médailles. Ivory.* 0,21 × 0,12 *m. Upper section:* Apollo and the Nine Muses. (Bibliothèque.)

55. Mycenaean Art. Goddess Enthroned. 14th-13th *century B.C. Athens, National Museum. Ivory. Height: about* 0,075 *m.* (Galerie de la Pléiade-Émile Séraf.)

56. Etruscan Art. *Vicinity of Ancona, Italy.* Goddess: Aphrodite (?). *Paris, Musée du Louvre. Bronze, with a block of lead beneath the feet. Height:* 0,33 *m.; head:* 0,022 *m.* (Tel-Vigneau.)

57. Colombian Art. Masculine Votive Figurine Called Tunjo. *Muiscal style. Bogotá, Museo del Oro. Height:* 0,15 *m.; maximum width:* 0,06 *m.; weight:* 33,9 *g.* (Museum.)

58. Sardinian Art. *Uta, Monti Arcosu.* Warrior Carrying a Sword and a Bow. *Period of the Nuraghi;* 7th *century B.C.* (?). *Cagliari, Archaeological Museum. Bronze. Height:* 0,24 *m.* (Galerie de la Pléiade.)

59. Etruscan Art. Mirror. Winged Victory in a Phrygian Cap. 3d-2d *century B.C. Paris, Musée du Louvre. Engraved bronze. Diameter:* 0.12 *m.* (Tel-Vigneau.)

60. Egytian Art. *Saqqara.* Woman Servant Milling Grain. *Old Empire.* 5th *dynasty. Cairo, Museum. Painted limestone. Height:* 0,35 *m. Document on the reverse side.* (Hassia.)

61. Greek Art. *Aegestratos,* coroplast *of Myrina.* Aphrodite. *Beginning of the* 2d *century B.C. Paris, Musée du Louvre. Terra cotta. Traces of colors. Height:* 0,25 *m.* (Galerie de la Pléiade-La Photothèque.)

62. Greek Art. *Thebes.* Seated Man Writing, *Last quarter of the* 6th *century B. C. Paris. Musée du Louvre. Terra cotta. Height:* 0,11 *m.* (Tel-Vigneau.)

63. Greek Art. *Athens. The painter is called* "*The Master of the triglyph.*" Lecythus with a White Background *(detail). Around* 400 *B.C. Athens, National Museum. Terra cotta. Height:* 0,57 *m.* (Galerie de la Pléiade-Émile Séraf.)

64. *Abbaye de Saint-Maurice d'Agaune ( Valais). Reliquary of St. Maurice (detail of one of the small sides).* The Virgin. *Whole of the reliquary:* 12th *century. The Virgin:* 13th *century. Natural or gilded silver; repoussé or niello work; precious stones. The face, the neck, and the hands of the Virgin were painted. Dimensions of the reliquary:* 0,798 × 0,357 *m. Height :* 0,575 *m. On the other, small side, as a counterpart to the Virgin, is a Christ giving blessing.* (Jaccard.)

65. Venice. Pala *(detail):* The Virgin in majesty. 12th-13th *century. Torcello, Provincial Museum. Tablets in repoussé silver, chased and gilded, placed on a wooden base. Total length:* 2,91 *m. Virgin in majesty:* 0,32 × 0,235 *m. This* pala *was originally composed of twenty-nine distinct*

pieces; there remain thirteen. *The Virgin in majesty is placed in the center.* (Osvaldo Böhm.)

66. Pala *(detail):* An Evangelist (?). 12th-13th *century. Caorle (Venezia), cathedral. Gold.* (Osvaldo Böhm.)

67. Annunciation of the Angel to Joseph. 12th *century. Rouen, Musée des Antiquités. Ivory.* 0,158 × 0,118 *m.* (Jean-Louis Ozanne.)

68. Byzantine Art. *Constantinople* (?). *Diptych panel, called* The Barberini Ivory *(detail):* An Emperor's Triumph. *Around A.D.* 500. *Paris, Musée du Louvre. Ivory. Dimensions of the whole:* 0,341 × 0,266 *m. Central panel:* 0,201 × 0,134 *m.* (Galerie de la Pléiade-La Photothèque.)

69. Assyrian Art. *Kalakh (Nimrod).* Ashurnasirpal Hunting the Lion *(detail).* 9th *century B.C. London, British Museum. Gypseous alabaster. Height:* 0,864 *m.* (Museum.)

70. Iranian Art. *Susa.* Cylinder seal. Walking lion. *Beginning of the* 3d *millennium B.C. Paris, Musée du Louvre. Stone. Height:* 0,046 *m.* (Tel-Vigneau.)

71. Romanesque Art. *Vézelay, west portal, tympanum:* The Pentecostal Christ *(detail).* 1125-1130. In situ. (Tel-Vigneau.)

72. Byzantine Art. *Triptych panel.* Christ Crowning the Empereor Roman II and the Empress Eudoxia *(detail). Around A.D.* 950. *Paris, Bibliothèque Nationale, Cabinet des Médailles. Ivory. Height:* 0,245 *m.* (Bibliothèque.)

73. Gothic Art. *The west face of the cathedral at Rheims, right-hand door, left splay.* St John the Baptist. *Around* 1230. In situ. (Jean Roubier).

74. Gothic Art. *Rheims.* St. John the Baptist *(detail).* (Jean Roubier.)

75. Gothic Art. *Bamberg (Bavaria), cathedral, east portal, or the portal of Adam, right splay.* Eve *(detail). Middle of the* 13th *century.* In situ. (Schneider-Lengyel.)

76. Gothic Art. *Bamberg (Bavaria), cathedral, east portal, or the portal of Adam, right splay* Adam *(detail). Middle of the* 13th *century.* In situ. (Schneider-Lengyel.)

77. IL ROSSO, GIAMBATTISTA DI JACOPO ROSSI (1494-1540). *Fontainebleau, château, Galerie François I.* Love Chastised by Venus for Having Abandoned Psyche *(detail).* In situ. *Mural painting.* (Galerie de la Pléiade-La Photothèque.)

78. *Le Maître du Roi René.* The Book of the Love-Stricken Heart. Love Entrusts to Desire the King's Heart. 1460-1470. *Vienna, National Library. Miniature.* (Galerie de la Pléiade-Draeger.)

79. POL DE LIMBOURG *or* POL MALOUEL *and his brothers* HENNEQUIN *and* HERMANN. Les Très Riches Heures du Duc de Berry. The Month of March: the Chateau at Lusignan *(detail). Around* 1414-1416. *Chantilly, Musée Condé. Miniature. Ten pages of this calendar are by the Limbourgs' hand; Jean Colombe de Bourges completed the eleventh page and executed the twelfth between* 1485 *and* 1489. (Draeger.)

80. *The Master of the Heures de Rohan.* Death Before His Judge. *Around* 1418-1425. *Paris, Bibliothèque Nationale. Miniature.* (Bibliothèque.)

81. Carolingian Art. *School of Rheims.* The Gospel Book of Ebbo, *Archbishop of Rheims.* St. Mark. *First half of the* 9th *century. Épernay, Bibliothèque municipale. Miniature.* 0,260 × 0,208 *m.* (Giraudon.)

82. Romanesque Art. *Tavant (Indre-et-Loire), église Saint-Nicolas, crypt.* The Virgin *(detail). First half of the* 12th *century.* In situ. *Mural painting.* (R.-G. Phelipeaux-Zodiaque.)

83. Romanesque Art. *School of the Loire. Angers, the abbey at Saint-Aubin.* Bible. *Christ. in majesty. End of the* 11th *century. Angers, Bibliothèque municipale. Miniature. Dimensions of the page:* 0,495 × 0,370 *m.* (Bibliothèque Nationale, Paris.)

84. Romanesque Art. *Montoire (Loir-et-Cher), priory of Saint-Gilles, chapel, east apse.* Christ in majesty. *First quarter of the* 12th *century.* In situ. *Mural painting.* (R.-G. Phelipeaux-Zodiaque.)

85. SIYAH KALEM. Battle of a Hero and a Demon 15th *century. Istanbul, Library of the Topkapi Palace. Miniature. Part of the album of Mehmed II the Conqueror.* (Haluk Doganbey.)

86. Irish Art. The Book of Kells. Virgin and Child. 8th *century. Dublin, Trinity College Library. Miniature.* 0,318 × 0,232 *m.* (Museum-The Green Studio.)

87. Romanesque Art. *The church at Saint-Benoît-sur-Loire, capital at the transept cross.* Discovery of the Remains of St. Benedict and of St. Scholastica. Christ *(detail).* 1026-1030. *Saint-Benoît-sur-Loire, Musée lapidaire*

de l'église, salle du Trésor. (R.-G. Phelipeaux-Zodiaque.)

88. Pre-Romanesque Art. The Pontifical of Winchester, *also* known as the Book of Offices of Archbishop Robert. Pentecost. *End of the* 10th *century*. *Rouen, Bibliothèque municipale*. *Miniature on parchment*. 0,325 × 0,238 *m*. (B. Lefebvre.)

89. Greek Art. *Delos, the house of masks*. Dionysius Riding a Panther. 2d *century B.C*. In situ. *Pavement mosaic. Semiprecious stones*; *onyx*. 1 × 1 *m*. (Galerie de la Pléiade-Émile Séraf.)

90. *Piazza Armerina (Sicily), villa Erculia, corridor of the Great Hunt, south apse*. Africa Between the Tiger, the Elephant, and the Phoenix. 4th *century. Pavement mosaic*. (Angelo Maltese, Syracuse.)

91. *Piazza Armerina (Sicily), villa Erculia, corridor of the Great Hunt*. The Great Hunt *(detail)*. 4th *century. Pavement mosaic. Dimensions of the whole:* 6 × 60 *m*. (Angelo Maltese, Syracuse.)

92. *Doura-Europos (Syria), temple of the Palmyran gods, naos, south wall*. The Great Sacrifice Scene *(detail):* Two Adolescents of the Conon Family. *Second half of the* 1st *century A.D. Damascus, Syria, Museum. Mural painting. Dimensions of the whole:* 4,35 × 3,80 *m*. (Manceau.)

93. *The cathedral at Chartres, north lattice, under the rose, at the center*. St. Anne Carrying the Virgin. *First half of the* 13th *century*. In situ. *Stained-glass window. Dimensions of the whole:* 7,47 × 1,70 *m*. (Draeger.)

94. *Studio known as "of Judith and Esther." Paris, Sainte-Chapelle, fourth south window*. Judith Bathing in the Fountains. *Around* 1243-1248. In situ. *Stained-glass window. Diameter:* 0,68 *m*. (Monuments historiques-Draeger.)

95. *The cathedral at Chartres, south side, first window of the choir aisle*. Notre-Dame de la Belle Verrière *(detail)*. Middle of the 12th *century*. In situ. *Stained-glass window. Dimensions of the whole:* 4,90 × 2,36 *m*. (Draeger.)

96. PAOLO DI DONO, *known as* PAOLO UCCELLO, (1397-1475). *Florence, Santa Maria del Fiore, dome*. The Resurrection of Christ. *Design:* 1443; *execution:* 1444 *(by Bernardo di Francesco)*. In situ. Stained-glass window. (Galerie de la Pléiade-Scala.)

97. Peruvian Art. *Paracas*. Cloak embroidered with a jaguar motif *(detail)*. *Necropolis culture*. *Around* 400-1000. *New York, the Brooklyn Museum. Cloth*. (Museum).

98. Coptic Art. *Antinoüs*. Horseman. 11th *century. Paris, Musée du Louvre. Wool tapestry*. 0,11 × 0,16 *m*. (Galerie de la Pléiade-Draeger.)

99. NICOLAS BATAILLE (master weaver). HENNEQUIN DE BRUGES (designer). The Apocalypse. An Angel Shows St. John the Whore of Babylon, Symbol of Idolatry and of All the Abominations. *Around* 1380. *Angers, château, Musée des Tapisseries. Tapistry. Present total length: around* 112 *m*. There remain seventy-seven fragments of the original 105. (Bruel.)

100. La dame à la licorne. The Sense of Smell. *Around* 1500. *Paris, Musée de Cluny. Tapestry*. 3,67 × 3,22 *m. Series of six tapestries representing the five senses, placed on either side of the "Lady."* (Galerie de la Pléiade-Draeger.)

101. TOMMASO DI GIOVANNI GUIDI, *known as* MASACCIO, (1401-1429). *Florence, Santa Maria del Carmine, Brancacci* chapel. Saint Peter. Baptizing *(detail)*. In situ. *Mural painting*. (Galerie de la Pléiade-Scala.)

102. Indian Art. *Ajanta, Cave II*. Birth of the Buddha. 6th *century*. In situ. *Mural painting*. (Archeological Survey of India.)

103. Indian Art. *Ellora, Cave XXI, porch, northwest pillar*. Goddess of the Ganges. 7th *century (begun around* 640, *completed after* 675). In situ. *(Time-Life Magazine, Eliot Elisofon.)*

104. Romanesque Art. *Berzé-la-Ville (Saône-et-Loire), Church of the Priory, apse*. The Martyrdom of St. Vincent. *Beginning of the* 12th *century*. In situ. *Mural painting*. (R.-G. Phelipeaux-Zodiaque.)

105. Romanesque Art. *Moissac, south portal, tympanum*. Christ in Majesty *(detail)*. 1110-1120. In situ. *Height of the Christ:* 2,42 *m. Height of the head, from the beard to the crown:* 0,47 *m*. (Yan-J. Dieuzaide.)

106. Art of Central Asia. *Kizil cave "of the painted pavement."* A Divinity and a Musician. 600-650. *Berlin, Staatliche Museen. Mural painting. Width:* 1,35 *m*. (Museum-Karl, Heinrich Paulmann.)

107. Japanese Art. *Nara, Horyu-ji Temple: Kondô, east wall*. Bodhisattva. *Second half of the* 7th *century. Mural painting*. 3,13 × 1,60 *m*.

This painting was destroyed by fire in 1949. (After Benri-Do.)

108. Greek Art. *Athens, Acropolis. Erechtheum.* Portico of the Caryatides *(southwest angle). Last quarter of the* 5th *century B.C. (around* 420). In situ. *Height of the statues:* 2,03 *m.* (Galerie de la Pléiade-Émile Séraf.)

109. Egyptian Art. *Gizeh.* The Great Sphinx and the Pyramid of Chephren. *Old Empire. Fourth dynasty.* In situ *The sphinx was hewn in a limestone quarry; the claws and forward parts of the torso are supported with hewn stone. Vestiges of red color on the face.* 20 × 57 *m., from the paws to the base of the tail. Pyramid: base:* 210,50 *m.; height:* 136,40 *m. Formerly:* 215,25 × 143,50 *m.* (Hassia.)

110. Sassanian Art. *Bishapur (Fars).* The investiture of Bahram I. *Second half of the* 3d *century (between* 273 *and* 276). In situ. (Roman Ghirshman.)

111. Indian Art. *Elephanta (Gulf of Bombay), Cave Temple.* The Mahesamurti Surrounded by Two Dvarapalas *(entrance guards).* 7th-8th *century. Post-Gupta style.* In situ. *Height:* 5,20 *m.* (Goloubev-Musée Guimet.)

112. Chinese Art. *Lung-Men (Honan, province). Temple of Fong-hien-sseu, Cave XIX.* Bodhisattva and Vaisravana *(guardian diety),* 672-675. In situ. *Gray limestone. Bodhisattva, height: around* 12 *m.* (Cl. Arthaud.)

113. Gothic Art. *Chartres, cathedral, Royal portal, left door, left splay.* Statue-columns. 1145-1150. In situ. (Roger Parry.)

114. Mexican Art. *Teotihuacan, Temple of Quetzalcoatl, west façade.* Head of the Plumed Serpent; *in the background, Pyramid of the Sun. Around* 300-650. In situ. (Bernard Villaret, Paris.)

115. Dogon Art. *Ogol village (Sanga region).* Mali. Fetish house. In situ. (Tony Saulnier.)

116. Khmer Art. Bayon (Angkor-Thom), Cambodia. Tower with Faces. *End of the* 12th, *beginning of the* 13th *century.* In situ. *Sandstone. On each tower four colossal faces represent Jayavarman VII, king and builder of Bayon, with the features of the Bodhisattva Lockesvara.* (Germain Krull.)

117. Chinese Art. *Tun-Huang, Cave* 205. The Buddha Surrounded by His Disciples *(detail).* 6th-7th *century.* In situ. *Painted clay.* (Cl. Arthaud.)

118. *Paris, Priory of Saint-Martin-des-Champs.* The Virgin and Child. *Third quarter of the* 12th *century. Basilica of Saint-Denis. Polychrome wood decorated with cabochons. Height:* 1,42 *m.* (Galerie de la Pléiade-La Photothèque.)

119. *Tyrolian artist* (?). Crucifixion *(detail). Before restoration. Second half of the* 12th *century (around* 1160-1180). Bologna, San Pietro. *Polychrome wood. Height of the crucifix:* 2,30 *m.* (Scala.)

120. *Tyrolian artist* (?). Crucifixion *(detail). After restoration.* (Scala.)

121. Catalonian Art. *Erill-la-Vall (Spain).* Descent from the Cross. 12th *century. Central part: Vich, Episcopal Museum; Virgin and St. John: Barcelona, Museum of Art of Catalonia. Wood (Mas.).*

122. Catalonian Art. *Mitgaran or Mig-Arán, Viella, chapel (Spain).* Torso of Christ. 12th *century. Viella, parish church. Polychrome wood.* 0,65 × 0,40 *m. On the Christ, which is part of a Descent from the Cross, one can still see the hand of Joseph of Arimathea.* (J. Dieuzaide-Zodiaque.)

123. Greek Art. *Athens.* Sphinx *(detail). Third quarter of the* 6th *century B.C. Athens, Museum of the Acropolis. Marble. Height:* 0,55 *m. Writing on the reverse.* (Galerie de la Pléiade-Emile Séraf.)

124. Egyptian Art. *Sakkara, serdab north of the step pyramid.* The Pharaoh Zoser *(detail). Old Empire.* 3d *dynasty. Cairo, Museum. Limestone. Traces of polychrome. Height:* 1,40 *m.* (Hassia.)

125. Greek Art. *Aegina, Temple of Aphaia, east fronton.* Head of Athena. *Around* 490 *B.C. Munich, Glyptothek und Museum Antiken Kleinkunst. Paros marble. Height:* 0,31 *m.* (Museum-F. Kaufman.)

126. Greek Art. *School of Rhodes.* Victory of Samothrace *(detail). Beginning of the* 2d *century B.C. (around* 190). Paris, Musée du Louvre. *Paros marble; galley; Rhodes limestone. Height:* 3,28 *m.* (Tel-Vigneau.)

127. Indian Art. *Khajuraho.* Nayika *(detail). Beginning of the* 11th *century.* In situ. *Stone.* (Archaeological Survey of India.)

128. Ancient Replica after PRAXITELES. The Venus of Cnidos. *Paris, Musée du Louvre. Marble. Height:* 1,22 *m.* (Galerie de la Pléiade-Draeger.)

129. Greek Art. *Attributed to* PYTHAGORAS OF RHEGIUM. *Delphi, Temple of Apollo.* The Charioteer *(detail). Around* 480-475 *B.C. Delphi, Museum. Bronze; eyes encrusted with enamel and with stones; lips with red copper; ornaments of the headband: silver and copper. Height:* 1,80 *m. The dedication gives the name of the donor: the tyrant Polyzelos of Gela (Sicily).* (Galerie de la Pléiade-Emile Séraf.)

130. Greek Art. PRAXITELES. Hermes *(detail). End of the* 4th *century B.C. (Around* 340*). Olympia, Museum. Paros marble. Height:* 2,15 *m.* (Giraudon.)

131. PIERO DI COSIMO, *or* DI LORENZO (1462-1521). The Death of Procris. *London. The National Gallery. Wood.* 0,65 × 1,83 *m.* (Museum-R. B. Fleming.)

132. NICCOLÓ DELL'ABBATE (1512-1571). The Abduction of Persephone *(detail). Paris, Musée du Louvre. Canvas. Dimensions of the whole:* 1,95 × 2,16 *m.* (Ina Bandy.)

133. HIERONYMUS VAN AEKEN, *known as* HIERONYMUS BOSCH, (*ca.* 1450/1460-1516). *Triptych.* The Temptation of St. Anthony *(detail of the central panel). Around* 1500. *Lisbon, Museu Nacional de Arte Antiga. Wood. Central panel:* 1,315 × 1,19 *m. Side panels:* 1,315 × 0,53 *m.* (Giraudon.)

134. REMBRANDT, HARMENSZ VAN RIJN (1606-1669). The Painter and His Model *(equally well known by the name of* Pygmalion*). Second state. Paris, Bibliothèque Nationale, Cabinet des Estampes. Etching.* 0,216 × 0,180 *m.* (Galerie de la Pléiade-La Photothèque.)

135. MICHELANGELO BUONARROTI (1475-1564). *Florence, San Lorenzo, Medici chapel (new sacristy).* 1520-1533. Tomb of Giuliano de Medici *(detail):* Night. In situ. *Marble. Length of the whole:* 1,94 *m.* (Galerie de la Pléiade-Scala.)

136. LEONARDO DA VINCI (1452-1519). St. Anne, the Virgin, and the Child *(detail).* 1506-1511. *Paris, Musée du Louvre. Wood. Dimensions of the whole:* 1,685 × 1,30 *m.* (Scala.)

137. REMBRANDT, HARMENSZ VAN RIJN (1606-1669). The Return of the Prodigal Son *(detail). Around* 1668-1669. *Signed. Leningrad, Hermitage Museum. Canvas.* 2,62 × 2,05 *m* (News Agency "Novosti.")

138. ERNEST MEISSONIER (1815-1891). French Campaign, 1814. 1864. *Signed and dated. Paris, Musée du Louvre. Wood.* 0,515 × 0,765 *m.* (Galerie de la Pléiade-Draeger.)

139. GEORGES ROUAULT (1871-1958). The Old King. 1937. *Signed. Pittsburgh, Museum of Art, Carnegie Institute. Canvas.* 0,77 × 0,54 *m.* (Museum-Elton L. Schnellbacher.)

140. Egyptian Art. *Sakkara.* The High Priest Renefer *(detail). Old empire.* 5th *dynasty. Cairo, Museum. Limestone. Traces of polychrome. Total height:* 1,80 *m.* (Hassia.)

141. Egyptian Art. Osiris. *Early period. Paris, Musée du Louvre. Painted and stuccoed wood; eyes encrusted with glass paste; scepters and crown ornaments: bronze. Height:* 1,59 *m.* (Galerie de la Pléiade-La Photothèque.)

142. NICOLÁS FRANCÉS (*ca* 1400-1468). Retable of the Virgin *(detail):* Scenes in the Life of St. Francis: St. Francis Surprised by the Thieves. *Madrid, The Prado.* (Galerie de la Pléiade-La Photothèque.)

143. ROGER VAN DER WEYDEN (*ca* 1400-1464). Retable of the Seven Sacraments. Central panel. *Anvers, Musée royal. Wood.* 2 × 0,97 *m.* (Scala.)

144. Indian Art. *School of the Mogols.* The Emperor Tamerlane on His Throne *(detail). Vienna, Schönbrunn chateau. Miniature. Decorates an* 18th*-century bedroom in the Schönbrunn chateau with other pages from an album.* (Schlosshauptmannschaft.)

145. REMBRANDT, HARMENSZ VAN RIJN (1606-1669). The Emperor Tamerlane on His Throne. 1654-1656. *Paris, Musée du Louvre. Japanese paper; Chinese pen and ink wash.* 0,186 × 0,187 *m. We know of twenty-three Rembrandt drawings made after Indian miniatures.* (Galerie de la Pléiade-La Photothèque.)

146. PICASSO, PABLO RUIZ (1881- ). Portrait of Ambroise Vollard. 1909-1910. *Moscow, Pushkin National Museum of Art. Canvas.* 0,92 × 0,65 *m.* (News Agency "Novosti.")

147. LEONARDO DA VINCI (1452-1519). St. John the Baptist *(detail). Around* 1509-1512. *Paris, Musée du Louvre. Wood.* 0,69 × 0,57 *m.* (Galerie de la Pléiade-Draeger.)

148. Head of a Young Saint. *Last quarter of the* 12th *century. Torcello, Provincial Museum. Mosaic.* 0,40 × 0,315 *m.* (Osvaldo Böhm.)

149. DIEGO RODRIGUEZ Y DE SILVA VELAZQUEZ (1599-1660). Las Meninas. 1656. *Madrid, The Prado. Canvas.* 3,18 × 2,76 *m.* (Anderson-Giraudon.)

150. PICASSO, PABLO RUIZ (1881- ). Las Meninas. *October* 3, 1957. *Private collection. Canvas.* 1,29 × 1,61 *m.* (Éd. Cercle d'Art.)

151. *Natural rock. Zurich, Rietberg Museum (Asian section).* (Museum.)

152. MICHELANGELO BUONARROTI (1475-1564). *Florence, San Lorenzo, Medici chapel (new sacristy).* The Medici Madonna *(detail).* In situ. *Marble. Height:* 2,26 *m.* (Galerie de la Pléiade-Scala.)

153. Catalonian Art. Madonna and Child *(detail).* 14th *century* (?), *Barcelona, Marès Museum. Painted wood. Height:* 0,77 *m.* (Galerie de la Pléiade-Mas.)

154. *Mali.* Masks. *(From* African Africa, *Lausanne, Éd. Clairefontaine,* 1963, *page* 117.)

155. Dogon Art *(Mali).* Mask representing an antelope. *Paris, Musée de l'Homme. Wood; the hair is braided fiber. Total height:* 1,30 *m. Writing on the reverse.* (Roger Parry.)

156. *School of Cologne.* The "Devout Christ" *(detail).* 1307. *Perpignan, Cathedral of St. John, Christ chapel. Holly wood. Height:* 1,64 *m. The date* 1307 *is given us by a parchment found on July* 4, 1952, *in a cavity in the back of the Christ that was made to hold relics.* (Raymond Gid-Pierre Jahan.)

157. GIAMBATTISTA DI JACOPO ROSSI, *known as* IL ROSSO, (1494-1540). Love Chastised by Venus for Having Abandoned Psyche. *Cf. fig.* 77. (Galerie de la Pléiade-La Photothèque.)

158. JEAN MARC NATTIER (1685-1766). Madame Adélaïde Tying Knots. 1756. *Signed and dated. Versailles, Pavillon de la Lanterne. Canvas.* 0,90 × 0,77 *m. This painting, at one time enlarged* (1,28 × 0,96 *m.) for placement above a door, has since regained its original dimensions.* (Galerie de la Pléiade-Draeger.)

159. JEAN MARC NATTIER (1685-1766). Madame Adélaïde Tying Knots. (Galerie de la Pléiade-Draeger.)

160. PAOLO CALIARI, *known as* PAOLO VERONESE, (1528-1588). *Venice, Convent of the Serviti.* The Feast in the House of Simon. *Before* 1573. *Versailles, Salon d'Hercule. Canvas.* 4,54 × 9,74 *m.* (Galerie de la Pléiade-La Photothèque.)

161. GEORGES BRAQUE (1882-1963). Seascape. *Paris, private collection. Canvas.* 0,50 × 0,95 *m.* (Galerie de la Pléiade-Draeger.)

162. Chinese Art. *Mask. Chang Dynasty.* 12th-14th *century B.C. (end of the Chang Dynasty). Chicago, The Art Institute (Buckingham Collection). Bronze. Gray-green patina. Height:* 0,220 *m. Width:* 0,361 *m. On the reverse side, an inscription gives the clan name of the man for whom the work was intended; above are two dragons facing each other.* (Museum.)

163. ALESSANDRO DI MARIANO FILIPEPI, *known as* SANDRO BOTTICELLI, (1444-1510). Venus and Mars. *Around* 1483. *London, The National Gallery. Wood.* 0,69 × 1,735 *m.* (Museum-R. B. Fleming.)

164. ERCOLE DE' ROBERTI (1456-1496). *Ferrare, Palazzo Schifanoia, room of the Months, northern wall, upper Section.* The month of September. The Loves of Mars and Venus *(detail). Finished in* 1478. In situ. *Mural painting. Dimensions of the room: length:* 24 *m.; width :* 11 *m. ; height:* 7,50 *m.* (Scala.)

165. Greek Art. *Athens, Acropolis.* Koré 686, *the Koré of Euthy dikos, also known as* La Boudeuse *(detail). Beginning of the* 5th *century B.C. (around* 500*). Athens, Acropolis Museum. Marble. Height:* 0,41 *m. The statue was dedicated by Euthydikos.* (Galerie de la Pléiade-Émile Séraf.)

166. Chichimec Art *(Mexico).* Head of a Serpent of the Sun. 14th *century.* In situ. *Basaltic stone. Height: around* 0,75 *m.* (Christian Baugey-Multiphoto.)

167. Dogon Art *(Mali).* Statuette. *Paris, private collection. Wood. Height:* 0,99 *m.* (Galerie de la Pléiade-Draeger.)

168 Romanesque Art. *Beauvais, église Saint-Lucien.* Head of a King. *End of the* 12th *century. Beauvais, Museum. Stone. Height:* 0,45 *m.* (Sougez.)

169. PICASSO, PABLO RUIZ (1881- ). The Reaper. 1943. *Private collection. Bronze. Height:* 0,50 *m.* (Brassaï.)

170. Greek Art. *School of Rhodes.* Victory of Samothrace. *Cf. fig.* 126. (Ina Bandy.)

171. Japanese Art. HAKUIN (1685-1763). Bonji: Sanskrit Character. Stylization of the Letter A. *Tokyo, private collection.* 0,108 × 0,056 *m. The calligraphy evokes the Beginning.* (Galerie de la Pléiade-Draeger.)

172. Indian Art. Elephanta *(Gulf of Bombay).* The Mahesamurti *(detail). Cf. fig.* 111. (Goloubev-Musée Guinet.)

THIS EDITION OF
*Museum Without Walls*
WAS PRINTED BY
IMPRIMERIE FIRMIN-DIDOT
PARIS-MESNIL-IVRY

imprimé en France.